IBM Cognos 8 Report Studio Cookbook

Over 80 great recipes for taking control of Cognos 8 Report Studio

Abhishek Sanghani

BIRMINGHAM - MUMBAI

IBM Cognos 8 Report Studio Cookbook

First published: May 2010

Production Reference: 1210510

Published by Packt Publishing Ltd.
32 Lincoln Road
Olton
Birmingham, B27 6PA, UK.

ISBN 978-1-849680-34-9

www.packtpub.com

Cover Image by Tina Negus (tina_manthorpe@sky.com)

Credits

Author
Abhishek Sanghani

Reviewers
Terry Curran
Marco Hartman
Sascha Mertens
Ramesh Parcha

Acquisition Editor
Rashmi Phadnis

Development Editor
Neha Patwari

Technical Editor
Neha Damle

Copy Editor
Sanchari Mukherjee

Editorial Team Leader
Gagandeep Singh

Project Team Leader
Lata Basantani

Project Coordinator
Joel Goveya

Proofreader
Lesley Harrison

Indexer
Hemangini Bari

Production Coordinator
Alwin Roy

Cover Work
Alwin Roy

About the Author

Abhishek Sanghani was born in India and attended Mumbai University where he majored in Computer Engineering. He began his career in 2004 as a Business Intelligence and Cognos Consultant, and has worked with leading IT and Finance Services companies since then.

He pursued Finance Management degree along with his work in the field of Cognos and BI, successfully progressing and winning awards and certifications year after year. Presently, he is working in the United Kingdom, utilizing his skills of Cognos, SQL, BI and Data Warehousing. In his free time, he writes technical blogs and also provides trainings/seminars on demand. This book is his first attempt in technical authoring.

Mail ID: abhishek.sanghani@gmail.com

Blog: http://biandcognos.blogspot.com/

I would like to thank the entire PACKT Publishing team for helping this endeavor. On the personal front, I am thankful to my loving wife Dolly for all the support, and my friend and work mate Amma Manso for all the valuable advice.

About the Reviewers

Terry Curran has worked in the IT industry for over 20 years after graduating from the University of Stirlling with an MSc in Software Engineering. He has considerable software development experience in many industries.

He has extensive knowledge of Cognos Reporting solutions, having worked with Cognos Business Intelligence software for a range of industries from Aviation to Pharmaceuticals over the past 10 years.

He is currently working as a freelance Cognos Business Intelligence consultant and contractor.

Marco Hartman is a Senior Business Intelligence Consultant, currently working at Imtech ICT Performance Solutions in the Netherlands.

He's working with Cognos products since 2004. Starting with Cognos PowerPlay and Impromptu, he now is an expert in the Cognos 8 platform. Marco is fully certified for Cognos 8 BI (Author, Modeler, Administrator, Scorecarding), Cognos 8 Planning and Cognos TM1. Besides Cognos, he also has experience with Business Objects and Microsoft SQL Server BI.

Marco works on different projects and customers. He is a qualified consultant who understands the needs of the customers. Besides his projects he is a trainer at IBM Cognos, Netherlands. He also likes to anticipate new developments.

Marco studied Business Administration at the Radboud University in Nijmegen and specialized in 'Knowledge and Information Management'. In his free time, he likes playing tennis and snowboarding.

Sascha Mertens graduated at the German University for Applied Sciences (HS Niederrhein) in 2001 as an engineer of economics. Focusing on the business part of his degree he began to work with Corporate Performance Management (CPM) topics in his thesis of 'Redesign of a controlling system by means of a management information system (MIS)'.

When starting to work for Deloitte in 2001 he was trained and certified in Analyst and Contributor by Adaytum—the original software producer—before they were acquired by Cognos and subsequently by IBM. With his gained knowledge, Sascha started to work for the first German Planning project with the Volkswagen Financial Services AG which was brought up to a status that is still alive today.

With the modeling of system designs and architectural concepts as well as their implementations into CPM systems, Sascha developed all kinds of planning models such as sales planning, cost planning, personnel planning etc, up to the resulting financial plans. Closely working together with Cognos, Sascha became a beta tester for several upcoming Planning releases and a community leader in one of the leading Cognos Planning forums on the internet.

With a strong focus on the conceptual and business side, he conducted a study for the 'State of planning within German companies' ('Standortbestimmung zur Planung in deutschen Unternehmen') and offered various public webcasts such as 'planning scenarios and simulations on board level', 'business planning for health insurance companies ', 'decentralized sales planning within the franchise industry', and 'driver based planning within a fleet management company'.

During his time with Deloitte Sascha made up his way to a senior managing level and designed and implemented Cognos Planning on a full-time basis in over 15 Cognos Planning and BI projects nationally, European and overseas in the last six years.

Since 2008, Sascha has been working for conunit, a consulting firm specialized on CPM and BI solutions and 'Cognos Partner of the year 2008 for Germany and Europe'. Within conunit Sascha and his team continue the Cognos Planning story with an offering of all kind of services around the IBM Cognos CPM and BI products including full scope projects (concept, design, and implementation), version upgrades and their migrations, as well as performance enhancements and system improvement checks.

It was a great pleasure reviewing this book. I am sure that it will be very helpful to you in setting up the Reporting system in your company. I would also like to thank people from Deloitte and Cognos that I worked with in collaborative projects who helped me in gaining the experience with the product.

Ramesh Parcha graduated in Mechanical Engineering from Gulbarga University in the year 1991.

After working for 7 years in Government Organization SETKHAM (Society for Training & Employment Promotion), Khammam, AP India, he worked for 4 Years in SIS Infotech Pvt ltd., Hyderabad, India.

He has also worked at the following places:

- Marketstrat Inc, Dublin, CA as a a Systems Engineer
- Minneapolis, MN as IDS (International Decision Systems)
- Virginia Department of Social Services, Richmond, VA as Sr Cognos Developer
- Tyco Fire & Building Products, Lansdale, PA as a BI and Web Developer
- Life Technologies, Carlsbad, CA as a Sr Cognos Consultant

I would like to thank Wilson D'souza and Joel Goveya.

Table of Contents

Preface

Cognos Report Studio is widely used for creating and managing business reports in medium to large companies. It is simple enough for any business analyst, power user, or developer to pick up and start developing basic reports. However, when it comes to developing more sophisticated, fully functional business reports for wider audiences, report authors will need guidance.

This book helps you to understand and use all the features provided by Report Studio to generate impressive deliverables. It will take you from being a beginner to a professional report author. It bridges the gap between the basic training provided by manuals or trainers and the practical techniques learned over years of practice.

What this book covers

Chapter 1, Report Authoring Basic Concepts, introduces you to some fundamental components and features that you will be using in most of the reports. This is meant to bring all readers on to the same page before moving on to advanced topics. It covers filters, sorting, aggregations, formatting, conditional formatting, and so on.

Chapter 2, Advanced Report Authoring, shows advanced techniques required to create more sophisticated report solutions that meet demanding business requirements. It covers cascaded prompts, master-detail queries, conditional block, defining drill links, and overriding the drill links. The most distinguishing recipe in this chapter is "Writing back to the database."

Chapter 3, Tips and Tricks: Java Scripts, shows how to manipulate the default selection, titles, visibility, and so on when the prompt page loads. It explains how to add programmability like validating the prompt selection before submitting the values to the report engine. A favorite recipe in this chapter is "Generating a bar chart using JavaScript". These recipes open a whole new avenue for you to progress on.

Chapter 4, Tips and Tricks: Report Page, shows some techniques to break boundaries and provides some features in reports that are not readily available in the Studio. It also talks about showing images dynamically (traffic lights), handling missing images, dynamic links to external website (for example, Google Maps), alternating drill links, showing tooltips on report, minimum column width and merged cells in Excel output.

Chapter 5, Xml Editing, shows you how to edit the report outside the Studio by directly editing the XML specifications. The recipes show you how to save time and quickly change references to old items, copy-paste the drill parameter mappings, and introduce you to important XML tags. The most intriguing recipe in this chapter is "A hidden gem in XML—row level formatting".

Chapter 6, Writing Printable Reports, gives you tips and shows you the options available within the Studio to make reports printable as business reports need to be printed and this part is often ignored during technical specification and development

Chapter 7, Working with Dimensional Models, When reports are written against a dimensional data source (or dimensionally modeled relational schema), a whole new style of report writing is needed. You can use dimensional functions, slicers, and others. Also, filtering and zero suppression are done differently. This chapter talks about such options (as dimensional data sources are becoming popular again).

Chapter 8, Macros, shows you that even though macros are often considered a Framework Modeler's tool, they can be used within Report Studio as well. These recipes will show you some very useful macros around security, string manipulation, and prompting.

Chapter 9, Using Report Studio Better, shows you the studio options and development practices to get the best out of Report Studio. It will include the understanding of Studio options, setting time-outs, capturing the real query fired on database, handling slow report validation, customizing classes, and so on.

Chapter 10, Some More Useful Recipes, is an assorted platter of useful recipes, meant to show more work-arounds, tricks, and techniques. A highlight recipe is–"changing style sheets at run time depending on the user".

Chapter 11, Best Practices, shows you how to achieve code commenting, version controlling, regression testing, and so on. It will also show you some useful practices you should cultivate as standard during development.

Appendix, Recommendations and References, covers topics that are very useful for a Cognos report developer such as version controlling, Cognos mash-up service, and Cognos Go Office.

What you need for this book

IBM Cognos Report Studio 8 (8.1 to 8.4).

Who this book is for

If you are a Business Intelligence or MIS Developer (programmer) working on Cognos Report Studio who wants to author impressive reports by putting to use what this tool has to offer, this book is for you. You could also be a Business Analyst or Power User who authors his own reports and wants to look beyond the conventional features of Report Studio 8.

This book assumes that you can do basic authoring, are aware of the Cognos architecture, and are familiar with Studio.

Conventions

In this book, you will find a number of styles of text that distinguish between different kinds of information. Here are some examples of these styles, and an explanation of their meaning.

Code words in text are shown as follows: "We can include other contexts through the use of the include directive."

A block of code is set as follows:

```
<script>
function img2txt(img) {
txt = img.alt;
img.parentNode.innerHTML=txt;}
</script>
```

When we wish to draw your attention to a particular part of a code block, the relevant lines or items are set in bold:

```
<script>
function img2txt(img) {
txt = img.alt;
img.parentNode.innerHTML=txt;}
</script>
```

New terms and important words are shown in bold. Words that you see on the screen, in menus or dialog boxes for example, appear in the text like this: "clicking the Next button moves you to the next screen".

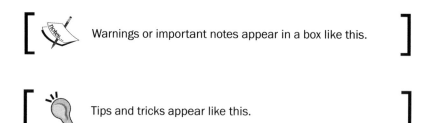

Warnings or important notes appear in a box like this.

Tips and tricks appear like this.

Reader feedback

Feedback from our readers is always welcome. Let us know what you think about this book—what you liked or may have disliked. Reader feedback is important for us to develop titles that you really get the most out of.

To send us general feedback, simply send an e-mail to feedback@packtpub.com, and mention the book title via the subject of your message.

If there is a book that you need and would like to see us publish, please send us a note in the SUGGEST A TITLE form on www.packtpub.com or e-mail suggest@packtpub.com.

If there is a topic that you have expertise in and you are interested in either writing or contributing to a book on, see our author guide on www.packtpub.com/authors.

Customer support

Now that you are the proud owner of a Packt book, we have a number of things to help you to get the most from your purchase.

Downloading the example code for the book

Visit https://www.packtpub.com//sites/default/files/downloads/0349_Code.zip to directly download the example code.

The downloadable files contain instructions on how to use them.

Errata

Although we have taken every care to ensure the accuracy of our content, mistakes do happen. If you find a mistake in one of our books—maybe a mistake in the text or the code—we would be grateful if you would report this to us. By doing so, you can save other readers from frustration and help us improve subsequent versions of this book. If you find any errata, please report them by visiting http://www.packtpub.com/support, selecting your book, clicking on the let us know link, and entering the details of your errata. Once your errata are verified, your submission will be accepted and the errata will be uploaded on our website, or added to any list of existing errata, under the Errata section of that title. Any existing errata can be viewed by selecting your title from http://www.packtpub.com/support.

Piracy

Piracy of copyright material on the Internet is an ongoing problem across all media. At Packt, we take the protection of our copyright and licenses very seriously. If you come across any illegal copies of our works, in any form, on the Internet, please provide us with the location address or website name immediately so that we can pursue a remedy.

Please contact us at copyright@packtpub.com with a link to the suspected pirated material.

We appreciate your help in protecting our authors, and our ability to bring you valuable content.

Questions

You can contact us at questions@packtpub.com if you are having a problem with any aspect of the book, and we will do our best to address it.

1
Report Authoring Basic Concepts

In this chapter, we will cover the following:

- ▸ The summary filter and detail filter
- ▸ Sorting options
- ▸ Aggregation and rollup aggregation
- ▸ Implementing `IF THEN ELSE` in filtering
- ▸ Data formatting options
- ▸ Creating sections
- ▸ Hiding columns in crosstab
- ▸ Examining display value and use value for prompts

Introduction

In this chapter, we will cover some fundamental techniques which will be used in your day-to-day life as a Report Studio author. In each recipe, we will take a real life example and see how it can be accomplished. At the end of the chapter, you will have learnt several concepts and ideas which you can mix-n-match to build complex reports.

Though this chapter is called 'Basic Concepts', it is not a beginner's guide or a manual. It expects the following:

- ▸ You are familiar with the Report Studio environment, components, and terminologies
- ▸ You know how to add items on the report page and open various explorers and panes
- ▸ You can locate the properties window and know how to test run the report

Based on my personal experience, I will suggest this chapter to new developers with two days to two months of experience. If you have larger experience with Report Studio, you might want to jump to the next chapter.

In the most raw terminology, a report is a bunch of rows and columns. The aim is to extract the right rows and columns from database and present them to the users. The selection of columns drive what information is shown in the report, and the selection of rows narrows the report to a specific purpose and makes it meaningful. The selection of rows is controlled by 'Filters'. Report Studio provides three types of filtering: **Detail, Summary**, and **Slicer. Slicers** are used with dimensional models and will be covered in later chapter (*Chapter 7, Working with Dimensional Models*). In the first recipe, we will cover when and why to use the **Detail** and **Summary** filter.

Once we get the correct set of rows by applying the filters, the next step is to present the rows in the most business-friendly manner. Grouping and ordering plays an important role in this. The second recipe will introduce you to the sorting technique for grouped reports.

With grouped reports, we often need to produce sub-totals and totals. There are various types of aggregation possible. For example, average, total, count, and so on. Sometimes the nature of business demands complex aggregation as well. In the third recipe, you will learn how to introduce aggregation without increasing the length of query. It will also show you how to achieve different aggregation for sub-totals and totals.

The fourth recipe will build upon the filtering concept you will have learnt earlier. It will talk about implementing IF THEN ELSE logic in filters. Then, we will see some techniques around data formatting, creating sections in a report, and hiding a column in crosstab.

Finally, the eighth and last recipe of this chapter will show you how to use prompt's **Use Value** and **Display Value** properties to achieve better performing queries.

The examples used in all the recipes are based on the **GO Data Warehouse** (**Query**) package which is supplied with Cognos 8.4 installation. These recipe samples can be downloaded from the Packt Publishing website. They use the relational schema from **Sales and Marketing | Sales (query)** namespace.

This is similar to Database Layer of the traditional GOSales package supplied with Cognos 8.2.

Please note that though there might be slight variations to scripts or features available in different versions of Report Studio, all the recipes mentioned in this book are applicable for all versions of Cognos 8 (8.1 through 8.4).

The screenshots used throughout this book are based on version 8.4. With versions 8.3 and 8.4, you need to choose **Professional Authoring Mode** from the **View** menu.

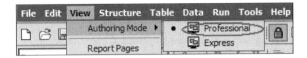

Summary filter and detail filter

Business owners need to see the sales quantity of their product lines to plan their strategy. They want to concentrate only on the highest selling product for each product line. They would also like the facility to select only those orders that are shipped in a particular month, for this analysis.

In this recipe, we will create a list report with product line, product name, and quantity as columns. We will create optional filter on Shipment Month Key. Also, we will apply correct filtering to bring only the highest sold product per product line.

Getting ready

Create a new list report based on GO Data Warehouse (query) package. From the Sales (query) namespace, bring **Product | Product Line**, **Product | Product Name**, and **Sales fact | Quantity** as columns.

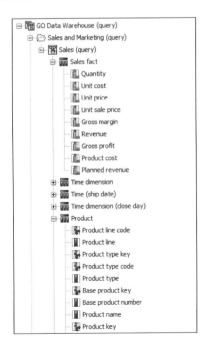

How to do it...

1. We will start with adding the optional filter on shipment month. To do that, click anywhere on the list report on Report Page. Select **Filters** from the toolbox.

2. In the **Filters** dialog box, add a new detail filter. Define filter as:
   ```
   [Sales (query)].[Time (ship date)].[Month key (ship date)] =
   ?ShipMonth?
   ```

3. Set the usage to **Optional**.

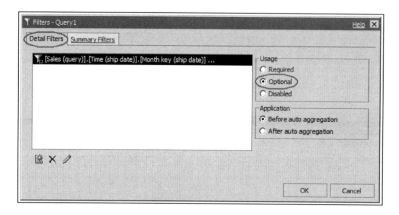

4. Now we will add a filter to bring only highest sold Product per Product line. To achieve this, select **Product line** and **Product name** (*Ctrl+select*) and click on the **Group** button from toolbox.

   This will create grouping shown as follows:

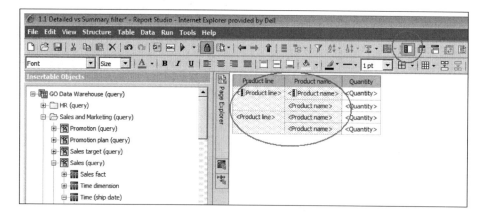

5. Now select the list and click on **Filter** button again. This time go to the **Summary filters** tab and add a new filter.

6. Define the filter as: `[Quantity] = maximum([Quantity] for [Product line])`.

7. Set usage to **Required** and set the scope to **Product name**.

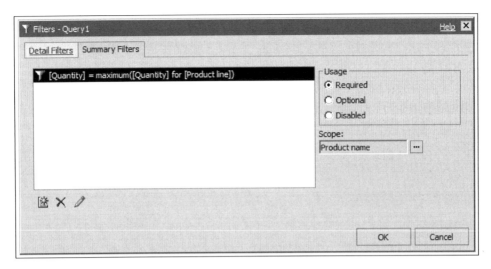

8. Now run the report to test the functionality. You can enter **200401** as **Month Key** as that has data in the Cognos supplied sample.

How it works...

Report Studio allows you to define two types of filters. Both work at different grain and hence have different applications.

Detail filter

The detail filter works at the lowest level of granularity in selected cluster of objects. In our example, this grain is the 'Sales entries' stored in the 'Sales fact'. By putting a detail filter on shipment month, we are making sure that only those sales entries which fall within the selected month are pulled out.

Summary filter

In order to achieve the highest sold product per product line, we need to consider the **aggregated sales quantity** for the products.

If we put a detail filter on quantity, it will work at sales entry level. You can try putting a detail filter of `[Quantity] = maximum([Quantity] for [Product line])` and you will see that it gives incorrect results.

So, we need to put a summary filter here. In order to let the query engine know that we are interested in filtering sales aggregated at product level, we need to set the **SCOPE** to **Product name**. This makes the query engine calculate `[Quantity]` at product name level and then allows only those product names where the value matches `maximum([Quantity] for [Product line])`.

There's more...

When you define multiple levels of grouping, you can easily change the scope of summary filters to decide the grain of filtering.

For example, if you need to show only those products whose sales are more than 1000 and only those product lines whose sales are more than 25000, you can quickly put two summary filters for [Quantity] with the correct **Scope** setting.

Before/After aggregation

The detail filter can also be set to apply after aggregation (by changing the **application** property). However, I think this kills the logic of detail filter. Also, there is no control on the grain at which the filter will apply. Hence, Cognos sets it to **before aggregation** by default, which is the most natural usage of the detail filter.

See also

Please read the "Implementing IF THEN ELSE in filtering" recipe in this chapter.

Sorting grouped values

The output of the previous recipe brings the right information back to the screen. It filters the rows correctly and shows highest selling product per product line for selected shipment month.

For better representation and to highlight the best selling product lines, we need to sort the product lines in descending order of quantity.

Getting ready

Open the report created in the previous recipe in Cognos Report Studio for further amendments.

How to do it...

1. Open the report in Cognos Report Studio.

2. Select the **Quantity** column.

3. Click on the **Sort** button from toolbar and choose **Sort Descending**.

4. Run the report to check if sorting is working. You will notice that sorting is not working.

5. Now go back to Report Studio, select **Quantity**, and click the **Sort** button again. This time choose **Advanced Sorting**.

6. Expand the tree for **Product line**. Drag **Quantity** from **Detail Sort List** to **Sort List** under **Product line**.

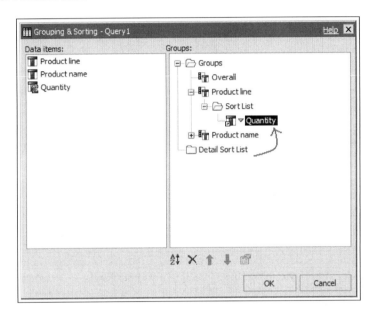

7. Click the **OK** button and test the report. This time the rows are sorted in descending order of **Quantity** as required.

How it works...

The Sort option by default works at the detailed level. This means the non-grouped items are sorted by the specified criteria within their own groups.

Here we want to sort the product lines which are grouped (not detailed items). In order to sort the Groups, we need to define the *advanced sorting option* as shown in this recipe.

There's more...

You can define it so for the whole list report from the Advanced Sorting dialog box. You can use different items and ordering for different groups and details.

You can also choose to sort certain groups by the data items that are not shown in the report. You need only bring those items from Source (model) to the Query, and you will be able to pick it in the sorting dialog.

Aggregation and rollup aggregation

Business owners want to see the unit cost of every product. They also want the entries to be grouped by product line and see the highest unit cost for each product line. At the end of the report, they want to see the average unit cost for the whole range.

Getting ready

Create a simple list report with **Product | Product line**, **Product | Product name** and **Sales Fact | Unit Cost** as columns.

How to do it...

1. We will start by examining the **Unit Cost** column. Click on this column and check the **Aggregate Function** property.
2. Set this property to **Average**.
3. Add grouping for **Product line** and **Product names**, by selecting those columns and hitting the **GROUP** button from toolbar.
4. Click on the **Unit Cost** column and click on the **Aggregate** button from toolbox. Select **Aggregate** option from the list.
5. Now click again on the **Aggregate** button and choose **Average** option.

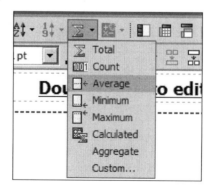

6. This will create footers shown as follows:

Product line	Product name	Unit cost
<▯Product line>	<▯Product name>	<Unit cost>
	<Product name>	<Unit cost>
<Product line>		**<Unit cost>**
<Product line>		**<Average(Unit cost)>**
<Product line>	<Product name>	<Unit cost>
	<Product name>	<Unit cost>
<Product line>		**<Unit cost>**
<Product line>		**<Average(Unit cost)>**
Summary		**<Unit cost>**
Summary		**<Average(Unit cost)>**

7. Now delete the line with **Average (Unit cost)** measure for Product line. Similarly, delete the line with **<Unit cost>** measure from **Summary**. The report should look like this:

Product line	Product name	Unit cost
<▯Product line>	<▯Product name>	<Unit cost>
	<Product name>	<Unit cost>
<Product line>		**<Unit cost>**
<Product line>	<Product name>	<Unit cost>
	<Product name>	<Unit cost>
<Product line>		**<Unit cost>**
Summary		**<Average(Unit cost)>**

8. Click on the **Unit cost** column and change its rollup aggregate function to **Maximum**.

9. Run the report to test it.

How it works...

In this recipe, we have seen two properties of the data items related to aggregation of the values.

Aggregation property

We first examined the aggregation property of unit cost and ensured that it is set to average. Remember that the unit cost here comes from the sales table. The grain of this table is sales entries or orders. This means there will be many entries for each product and their unit cost will repeat.

We want to show only one entry for each product and the unit cost needs to be rolled up correctly. The aggregation property determines what value is shown for unit cost when calculated at product level. If it is set to TOTAL, it will wrongly add up the unit costs for each sales entry. Hence, we are setting it to AVERAGE. It can be set to MINIMUM or MAXIMUM depending on business requirements.

Rollup aggregation

In order to show the MAXIMUM unit cost for product type, we create an 'Aggregate' type of footer in step 4 and set the **Rollup Aggregation** to **Maximum** in step 8.

Here we could have directly selected MAXIMUM from the 'Aggregate' drop-down toolbox. But that creates a new data item called **Maximum (Unit Cost)**. Instead, we ask Cognos to aggregate the number in footer and drive the type by rollup aggregation property. This will reduce one data item in the Query Subject and Native SQL.

Multiple aggregations

We also need to show the overall average at the bottom. For this we have to create a new data item. So, we selected unit cost and created an 'Average' type of aggregation in step 5. This calculates the Average (Unit Cost) and places it on the product line and in the overall footer.

We then deleted the aggregations that are not required in step 7.

There's more...

The rollup aggregation of any item is important only when you create the aggregation of 'Aggregate' type. When it is set to automatic, Cognos will decide the function based on data type which is not preferred.

It is good practice to always set the aggregation and rollup aggregation to meaning function than leaving as 'automatic'.

Implementing IF THEN ELSE in filters

Business owners want to see the sales quantity by order methods. However, for the 'Sales Visit' type of order method, they want a facility to select the retailer.

Therefore, the report should show quantity by order methods. For the order methods other than 'Sales Visit', the report should consider all the retailers. For 'Sales Visit' orders, it should filter on the selected retailer.

Getting ready

Create a simple list report with **Order Method | Order Method** and **Sales Fact | Sales Quantity** as columns. Group by order method to get one row per method and set the aggregation for quantity to **TOTAL**.

How to do it...

1. Here we need to apply the retailer filter only if Order Method is 'Sales Visit'. So, we start with adding a new detail filter.

2. Define the filter as: `if ([Order method]='Sales visit') then ([Sales (query)].[Retailer site].[Retailer name] = ?SalesVisitRetailer?)`

3. Validate the report. You will find multiple error messages.

4. Now change filter definition to this: `((([Order method]='Sales visit') and ([Sales (query)].[Retailer site].[Retailer name] = ?SalesVisitRetailer?)) or ([Order method]<>'Sales visit')`

5. Validate the report and it will be successful.

6. Run the report and test the data.

How it works...

The `IF ELSE` construct works fine when it is used in data expression. However, when we use it in a filter, Cognos often doesn't like it. It is strange because the filter is parsed and validated fine in the expression window and `IF ELSE` is a valid construct.

The workaround for this problem is to use the pair of `AND..OR` as shown in this recipe. The `IF` condition and corresponding action item are joined with `AND` clause. The `ELSE` part is taken care by `OR` operations with the reverse condition (in our example, `Order Method <> 'Sales Visit'`).

There's more...

You need not use both `AND` and `OR` clauses all the time. The filtering in this example can also be achieved by this expression:

```
([Sales (query)].[Retailer site].[Retailer name] = ?SalesVisitRetailer?)
```

or

```
([Order method]<>'Sales visit')
```

Depending on the requirement, you need to use only OR, only AND, or the combination of AND..OR.

Make sure that you cover all the possibilities.

Data formatting options: Dates, numbers, and percentages

Virtually all the reports involve displaying numerical information. It is very important to correctly format the numbers. In this recipe, we will create a report which formats dates, numbers, and percentages.

Date transformation and formatting are important in business reports. We will see two ways of displaying **MONTH-YEAR** from the 'Shipment Date Key'. We will apply some formatting to a numeric column and will also configure a ratio to be displayed as percentage.

Getting ready

Create a simple list report with **Product | Product line**, **Product | Product type** and **Time (Ship date) | Day key (Ship date)** as columns from the **Sales (query)** namespace.

Also add **Quantity**, **Unit Price**, and **Unit Cost** from the **Sales Fact Query Subject**.

Create grouping on **Product line** and **Product type**.

How to do it...

1. We will start by adding a new calculation to convert the **Shipment Day Key** into a date and show in **MONTH-YEAR** format. So, add a new **Query Calculation** to the report from the toolbox.

2. Define the calculation as: `cast([Sales (query)].[Time (ship date)].[Day key (ship date)], date)`.

3. Select this new column for the calculation and open **Data Format** from Properties pane. Open the **Data Format** dialog by clicking on the browse button next to **Data Format** property.

4. Choose the format type Date, set Date Style to Medium, and set **Display Days** to **No**.

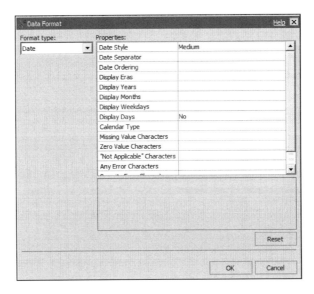

5. Now select the **Quantity** column on the report. Choose **Data Format** from property and open the dialog again.

6. This time pick 'Number' as the type and set different properties as required. In our example recipe, we will set the number of decimal points to 2, and use brackets () as a negative sign symbol.

7. Finally, we will add the ratio calculation to report. For that, add a new query calculation and define it as: [Unit price]/[Unit cost].

8. Select this column and from **Data Format** property dialog, set it as **Percent**. Choose % as the percent symbol and set the number of decimal places to 2. Also set the **Divide by Zero Characters** to N/A.

9. Run the report to test it.

How it works...

In this recipe, we are trying multiple techniques. We are using the CAST function to convert a number to date. Also, we are checking how dates can be formatted to hide certain details (for example, days) and how to change the separator. Finally, we have tested formatting options for numbers and percentage.

CAST function

The CAST function is used to convert data from one format to another. We specify the target format in second argument. Here, we are converting to date. It converts the date key which is in YYYYMMDD format to a date.

Later, we are setting the data format for this column as date for display purpose. We have set the display days to **No** as we only want to display MONTH-YEAR.

Numerical format

This is straightforward. The quantity column is displayed with two decimal points and negative numbers are displayed in brackets as this is what we have set the data formatting to.

% Margin

The ratio of unit price to unit cost is calculated by this item. Without formatting, the value is simply the result of *division operation*. By setting the data format to **Percent**, Cognos automatically multiplies the ratio by 100 and displays it as percentage.

There's more...

Please note that ideally the warehouse stores a calendar table with a 'Date' type of field , or this is made available through Framework Model. So, we need not cast the key to date every time. However, this recipe is meant to show you the technique and introduce you to the casting function.

Also, we are assuming here that business needs to see the shipment month. So, they want to see MONTH YEAR format only and we are hiding the days.

Another way of achieving this is explained as follows:

Let us change the expression for **Shipment Day Key** column to this: [Sales (query)]. [Time (ship date)].[Day key (ship date)]/10000

Now set the **Data Format** to **Number**, with the following options:

- ▸ No of decimal places = 2
- ▸ Decimal separator = hyphen (-)
- ▸ Use thousand separator = No

Run the report to examine the output. You will see that we have gotten rid of the last two digits from the day key and the year part is separated from month part by a hyphen. This is not truly converted to MONTH YEAR but conveys the information.

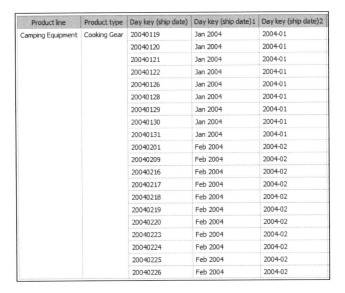

The advantage here is that the numerical operation is faster than CAST to DATE. We can use similar techniques to cosmetically achieve the required result.

Creating sections

Users want to see the details of **Orders**. They would like to see the **Order number** and the details (product name, promotion, quantity, and unit sell price).

Getting ready

Create a simple list report with **Sales order | Order number**, **Product | Product name**, **Sales fact | Quantity**, and **Sales fact | Unit sale** price as columns.

How to do it...

1. Click on the **Order number** column. Hit the section button on the toolbar.

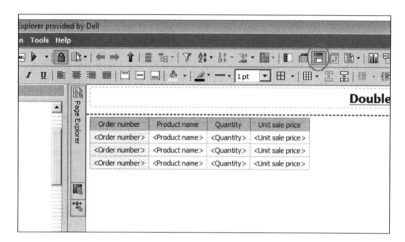

2. You will see that Report Studio automatically creates a header for **Order number** and moves it out of the list.

3. Notice that the **Order number** field is now grouped.

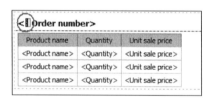

4. Run the report to test it.

How it works...

The information we are trying to show in this report can also be achieved by normally grouping on order number. That will bring all the related records together. We can also set appropriate group/level span and sorting for better appearance.

However, in this recipe, I want to introduce another feature of Report Studio called **Section**.

When you create a section on a column, Report Studio automatically does the following:

1. It creates a new list object and moves the current report object (in our case, the existing list) inside that. This is report nesting. Both the inner and outer objects use the same query.

2. It creates grouping on the column selected for section, which is **Order Number** here. Creates a **Group Header** for that item and removes it from the inner list.

3. It formats to outer list appropriately. For example, hiding the column title.

There's more...

Some of the advantages of creating sections are as follows:

1. As mentioned above, Report Studio does a lot of the work for you and gives a report that looks more presentable. It makes the information more readable by clearly differentiating different entities, in our case, different orders.

2. As the outer and inner queries are same, there is no maintenance overhead.

See also

If you create a section for a crosstab or chart report, you need to explicitly define the master-detail relationship. Chapter 2 defines the master-detail relationship.

Hiding column in crosstab

Users want to see sales figures by periods and order method. We need to show monthly sales and year's totals. The year should be shown in the **Year total** row and not as a separate column.

Getting ready

Create a crosstab report with **Sales fact | Quantity** as a measure. Drag **Time dimension | Current year** and **Month** on rows, **Order method | Order method** on column as shown in the following screenshot. Create aggregation on measure.

Quantity		<#Order method#>	<#Total(Order method)#>
<#Current year#>	<#Month#>	<#1234#>	<#1234#>
	<Current year>	<#1234#>	<#1234#>
<#Total(Current year)#>		<#1234#>	<#1234#>

Define appropriate sorting.

How to do it...

1. First, let's identify the issue. If you run the report as it is, you will notice that the year is shown to the left of the months. This consumes one extra column. Also, the yearly total doesn't have user friendly title.

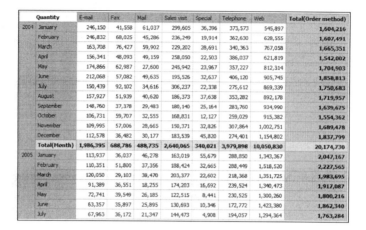

Quantity		E-mail	Fax	Mail	Sales visit	Special	Telephone	Web	Total(Order method)
2004	January	246,150	41,558	61,037	299,605	36,396	373,573	545,897	1,604,216
	February	246,832	68,025	45,286	236,249	19,914	362,630	628,555	1,607,491
	March	163,708	76,427	59,902	229,202	28,691	340,363	767,058	1,665,351
	April	156,341	48,093	49,159	258,050	22,503	386,037	621,819	1,542,002
	May	174,866	62,987	27,600	245,942	23,967	357,227	812,314	1,704,903
	June	212,068	57,082	49,635	195,526	32,637	406,120	905,745	1,858,813
	July	150,439	92,102	34,616	306,237	22,338	275,612	869,339	1,750,683
	August	157,927	51,939	40,620	186,373	37,638	353,282	892,178	1,719,957
	September	148,760	37,378	29,483	180,140	25,164	283,760	934,990	1,639,675
	October	106,731	59,707	32,555	168,831	12,127	259,029	915,382	1,554,362
	November	109,995	57,006	28,665	150,371	32,826	307,864	1,002,751	1,689,478
	December	112,578	36,482	30,177	183,539	45,820	274,401	1,154,802	1,837,799
	Total(Month)	1,986,395	688,786	488,735	2,640,065	340,021	3,979,898	10,050,830	20,174,730
2005	January	113,937	36,037	46,278	163,019	55,679	288,850	1,343,367	2,047,167
	February	110,351	51,800	37,356	188,424	32,665	288,449	1,518,520	2,227,565
	March	120,050	29,103	38,470	203,377	22,602	218,368	1,351,725	1,983,695
	April	91,389	36,551	18,255	174,203	16,692	239,524	1,340,473	1,917,087
	May	72,741	39,549	26,185	122,515	8,441	230,525	1,300,260	1,800,216
	June	63,357	35,897	25,895	130,693	10,346	172,772	1,423,380	1,862,340
	July	67,963	36,172	21,347	144,473	4,908	194,057	1,294,364	1,763,284

2. We will start by updating the title for yearly total row. Select **<Total(Month)>** crosstab node. Change its **Source type** to **Data item value** and choose **Current year** as the **Data item**.

3. Run the report and check that the yearly total is shown with the appropriate year.

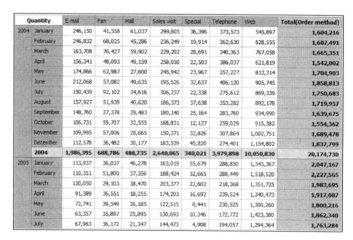

Quantity		E-mail	Fax	Mail	Sales visit	Special	Telephone	Web	Total(Order method)
2004	January	246,150	41,558	61,037	299,605	36,396	373,573	545,897	1,604,216
	February	246,832	68,025	45,286	236,249	19,914	362,630	628,555	1,607,491
	March	163,708	76,427	59,902	229,202	28,691	340,363	767,058	1,665,351
	April	156,341	48,093	49,159	258,050	22,503	386,037	621,819	1,542,002
	May	174,866	62,987	27,600	245,942	23,967	357,227	812,314	1,704,903
	June	212,068	57,082	49,635	195,526	32,637	406,120	905,745	1,858,813
	July	150,439	92,102	34,616	306,237	22,338	275,612	869,339	1,750,683
	August	157,927	51,939	40,620	186,373	37,638	353,282	892,178	1,719,957
	September	148,760	37,378	29,483	180,140	25,164	283,760	934,990	1,639,675
	October	106,731	59,707	32,555	168,831	12,127	259,029	915,382	1,554,362
	November	109,995	57,006	28,665	150,371	32,826	307,864	1,002,751	1,689,478
	December	112,578	36,482	30,177	183,539	45,820	274,401	1,154,802	1,837,799
	2004	1,986,395	688,786	488,735	2,640,065	340,021	3,979,898	10,050,830	20,174,730
2005	January	113,937	36,037	46,278	163,019	55,679	288,850	1,343,367	2,047,167
	February	110,351	51,800	37,356	188,424	32,665	288,449	1,518,520	2,227,565
	March	120,050	29,103	38,470	203,377	22,602	218,368	1,351,725	1,983,695
	April	91,389	36,551	18,255	174,203	16,692	239,524	1,340,473	1,917,087
	May	72,741	39,549	26,185	122,515	8,441	230,525	1,300,260	1,800,216
	June	63,357	35,897	25,895	130,693	10,346	172,772	1,423,380	1,862,340
	July	67,963	36,172	21,347	144,473	4,908	194,057	1,294,364	1,763,284

4. Now, we need to get rid of the year column on left edge. For that, click the **Unlock button** 🔒 on Report Studio toolbar. The icon should change to an open lock (unlocked).

5. Now select the <#Current Year#> text item and delete it.

6. Select the empty crosstab node left after deleting the text. Change its padding to 0 pixels and font to 0.001 pt size.

7. Run the report.

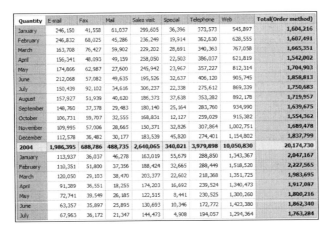

As you can see the year column on the left is now successfully hidden.

How it works...

When we want to hide an object in Report Studio, we often set its **Box Type** property to **None**. However, in this case, that was not possible.

Try setting the box type of year column to **None** and run the report. It will look like the following screenshot:

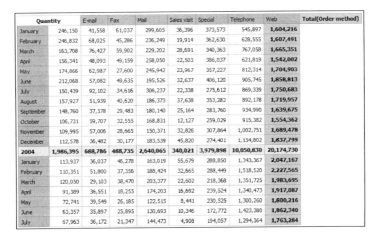

As you can see, the cells have shifted to the left leaving the titles out of sync. This is most often the problem when Report Studio creates some *merged* cells (in our case, for the aggregations).

The solution to this is to format the column in such a way that it is hidden in the report.

There's more...

This solution works best in HTML output. The excel output still has a column on the left with no data in it.

You might need to define the background colour and bordering as well, so as to blend the empty column with either the page background on left or the month column on right.

Prompts: Display value versus use value

In order to achieve the best performance with our queries, we need to perform filtering on the numerical key columns. However, the display values in the prompts need to be textual and user friendly.

In this recipe, we will create a filter that displays the product line list (textual values) but actually filters on the numerical codes.

Getting ready

Create a simple list report with **Product | Product name** and **Sales fact | Quantity** as columns.

How to do it...

1. Open Page Explorer and click on the **Prompt Pages** folder. Drag a new page from **Insertable Objects** under **Prompt Pages**.

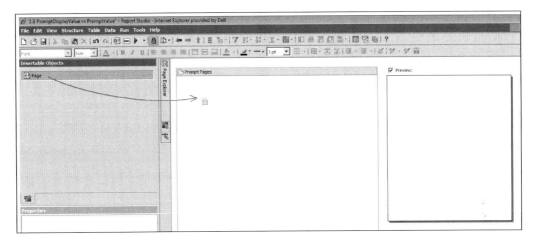

2. Double click on the newly created prompt page to open it for editing.

3. From **Insertable Objects**, drag **Value Prompt** to the prompt page. This will open a wizard.

4. Set the prompt name to ProductLine, and then click Next.

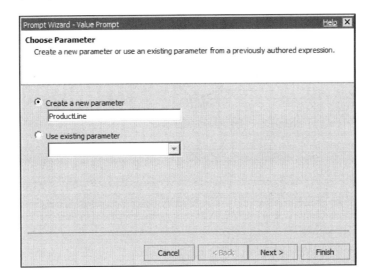

5. Keep the **Create a parameterized filter** option checked. For package item, choose **Sales (query) | Product | Product line code**. Click **Next**.

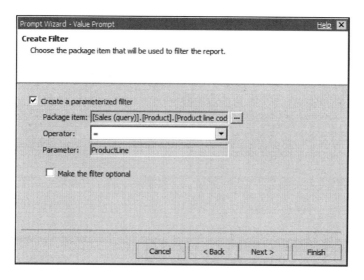

6. Keep **Create new query** option checked. Give the query name as **promptProductLine**.

7. Under **Value to display** select **Sales (query) | Product | Product line**.

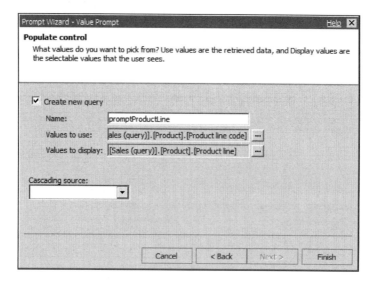

8. Click the **Finish** button. Run the report to test it.

How it works...

When you drag a prompt object from insertable objects, Report Studio launches the prompt wizard.

In the first step, you choose the parameter to be connected to the prompt. It might be an existing parameter (defined in query filter or framework model) or a new one. In this recipe, we chose to create a new one.

Then, you are asked whether you want to create a filter. If there is already a filter defined, you can uncheck this option. In our example, we are choosing this option and creating a filter on **Product line code**. Please note that we have chosen the *numerical key column* here. Filtering on a numerical key column is standard practice in data warehousing as it improves the performance of the query and uses the index.

In next step, Report Studio asks where you want to create a new query for prompt. This is the query that will be fired on database to retrieve prompt values. Here we have the option to choose a different column for display value.

In our recipe, we chose **Product line** as display value. Product line is the textual or descriptive column that is user friendly. It has one to one mapping with the **Product line code**. For example, Camping Equipment has Product Line Code of 2101.

Hence, when we run the report, we see that the prompt is populated by Product line names, which makes sense to the users. Whereas if you examine the actual query fired on the database, you will see that filtering happens on the key column, that is, **Product line code**.

There's more...

You can also check the 'Generated SQL' from Report Studio.

For that, select the **Tools | Show Generated SQL/MDX** option from the menu.

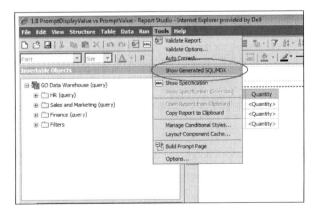

It will prompt you to enter a value for the product line code (which is proof that it will be filtering on the code).

Enter any dummy number and examine the query generated for the report. You will see that the product line code (key column) is being filtered for the value you entered.

So, now you know how the 'Prompt display values' and 'Use values' work.

If you ever need to capture the prompt value selected by the user in expressions (which you will often need for conditional styling or drill-throughs), you can use the following two functions.

- ▶ **ParamDisplayValue (parameter name)**: This function returns the textual value which represents the display value of the prompt. In our example, it will be the product line that was selected by the user.

- ▶ **ParamValue(parameter name)**: This function returns the numeric value which represents the use value of the prompt. In our example, it will be the Product Line Code for the Product Line selected by the user.

2
Advanced Report Authoring

In this chapter, we will cover the following:

- ▶ Adding cascaded prompts
- ▶ Nested reports: defining master detail queries
- ▶ Writing back to the database
- ▶ Conditional formatting
- ▶ Show negative numbers in red and brackets
- ▶ New conditional styling with version 8.3 onwards
- ▶ Conditional block—many reports in one
- ▶ Drill link from crosstab intersections
- ▶ Overriding crosstab intersection expression and drill

Introduction

Now as you have implemented the recipes in Chapter 1, or read them through, I am confident that we are on the same page about fundamental techniques of report authoring.

You now know how filtering, sorting, and aggregations work. You also know how to apply data formatting, create sections, and hide columns. You are also now aware of how to add new prompts and select appropriate options in the prompt wizard.

Based on this understanding, we will now move on to some advanced topics; including cascaded prompts, nested reports, and conditional blocks. We will also examine some techniques around drill-through links. These will enable you to create professional reports as required in current industrial environments.

Adding a cascaded prompt

Business owners want to see sales made by employees. They also want the facility to limit the report to certain region, country, or employee.

When they select a region, they would like the country pick-list to automatically reduce to the countries falling in that region. Similarly, the employee pick-list should also reduce when they pick a country.

Getting ready

Create a simple list report with **Employee name** (from **Employee by region** query subject) and **Quantity** (from **Sales fact**).

Define appropriate grouping and sorting for **Employee name** and ensure that aggregations for **Quantity** are correctly set.

How to do it...

1. We will start by creating detailed filters on the report query. Select the list report and open the filters dialog by clicking the **Filters** button.

2. Add three detailed filters as follows:

   a. `[Employee name]=?Employee?`

   b. `[Sales (query)].[Employee by region].[Country]=?Country?`

   c. `[Sales (query)].[Employee by region].[Region]=?Region?`

3. Define all filters as **Optional**.

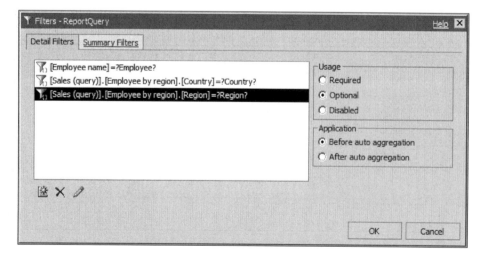

32

4. Now create a new prompt page. We will start by adding a prompt for **Region**.

5. Drag a new value prompt. In the prompt wizard, choose the existing parameter **Region** for it. Choose to create a new query called **Regions** for this parameter.

6. Click the **Finish** button.

7. Now add another value prompt. Choose the existing parameter **Country** for this, and create a new query called **Countries**. On the same page, choose **Region** under the **Cascading source**.

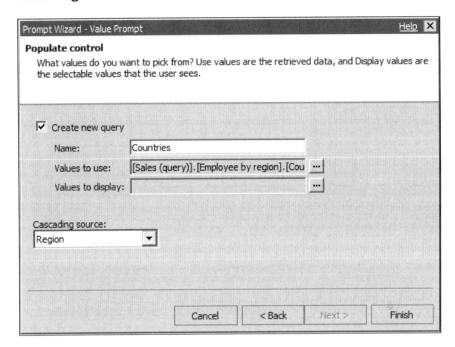

8. Similarly, add third and last value prompt for employee. Choose **Employee** as a parameter, **Employees** as the query name, and **Country** for the **Cascading source**.

9. Select the **Region** prompt and set its **Auto-Submit** property to **Yes**. Do the same for the **Countries** prompt.

10. Run the report to test it.

How it works...

In our case, users may run the report for the whole company, select particular region, select a region and country combination, or go all the way down to employees. We want to allow them to submit the selections at any stage. That is why we created three filters and kept them all optional.

Even if it was mandatory for the users to select an employee, we would have kept filters for country and region. The reason is that one employee might have done sales for different countries/regions. By keeping those filters, we would assure that report fetches data for that employee, for the selected Region/Country only.

Cascaded source

When we set the **Cascaded source** property, Report Studio ensures two things. Firstly, the prompt is disabled until the cascaded source is satisfied. Secondly, when re-prompted and the cascade source is populated, the prompt values are filtered accordingly.

In our case, the countries prompt remains disabled until a valid value for region is submitted. Similarly, employee list is disabled until a valid value is submitted for countries.

There's more...

In step 9, we set the **Auto-Submit** property to **Yes** for the prompts.

Auto submit

When the auto-submit property is set to **Yes**, the prompt value is automatically submitted when the user selects one. This enables the dependant prompt to be correctly filtered and enabled.

In our recipe, auto-submit for **Region** is set to **Yes**. Hence, when you select a region, the value is automatically submitted and the **Country** prompt is enabled with the correct values populated.

This action can also be performed by a **Reprompt** button. In that case, auto-submit is not required. This will be covered in detail in the next recipe.

More info

Up to version 8.2, when a prompt value is submitted by an auto-submit action, the whole page refreshes. You can see the progress bar in the browser become active and the page takes a few moments to reappear.

With version 8.3, a new technology is implemented in Cognos. The auto-submit action does not reload the whole page. Instead, only affected prompts are refreshed. This action is much quicker and gives a seamless experience to users.

See also

This recipe assumed that you are aware of the Prompt Wizard options. If not, please refer to Chapter 1, recipe '**DisplayValue versus UseValue**'.

Creating nested report: Defining master detail relationship

Users want to see product lines, products, and corresponding unit costs. For every product, they also want to see the trend of sales over last year.

We need to produce a list report with required information and nest a line chart within it to show the sales trend.

Getting ready

Create a simple list report based on the Sales (query) namespace. Pull **Product | Product line**, **Product | Product name** and **Sales fact | Unit cost** in the list.

How to do it...

1. We already have a list report that shows the product lines, products, and corresponding unit costs. Please make sure that appropriate sorting and aggregations are applied to the columns.

2. Now we will add a nested **Chart** object to show the sales trend for each product.

3. Drag a new **Chart** object from the **Insertable Objects** pane onto the report as a column.

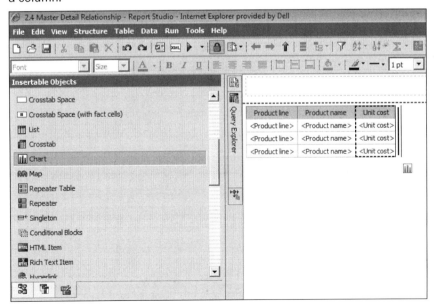

4. Choose an appropriate chart type. In this recipe, we will choose "Line with Markers".

5. From Source pane, drag **Quantity** from **Sales fact** onto the chart as the **Default measure**. Drag **Month key** from time dimension under **Category** and **Product name** from product dimension as the **Series**.

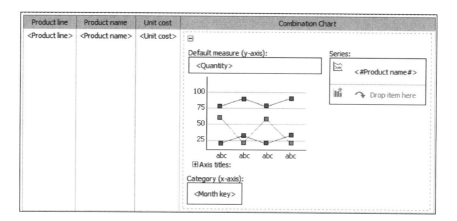

 Please note that we are using the month key here in order to show the monthly figures in correct order. You can later on use a category label to show month names. Directly pulling the month name results in alphabetic sorting, and hence in an incorrect trend.

6. Now click anywhere on the chart and choose **Data | Master Detail Relationship** from the menu bar.

7. Create a new link and connect **Product name** items from both the queries.

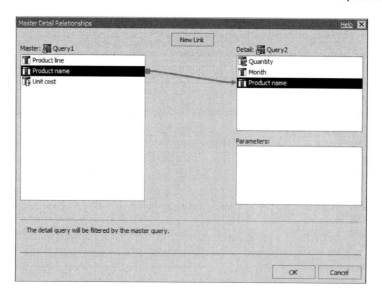

8. Click the **OK** button to come back on the Report Page. Now select the **Y1 Axis** of chart by clicking on it.

9. Change its **Use Same Range for All Instances** property to **No**.

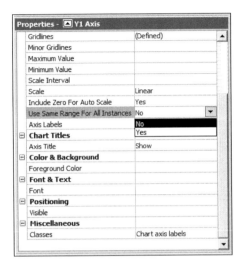

10. Now click on the **Chart** and click the **Filter** button from toolbar.

11. Define a detailed filter on **Current** Year from time dimension as required. In this recipe, I will hard code it to **2004**. So, the filter is defined as: `[Sales (query)].[Time dimension].[Current year]=2004`.

    Though in practical cases, you would have to filter for year, rather than hard-coding.

12. Run the report to test it.

13. Update the chart properties (size, marker, color, and so on) for better presentation.

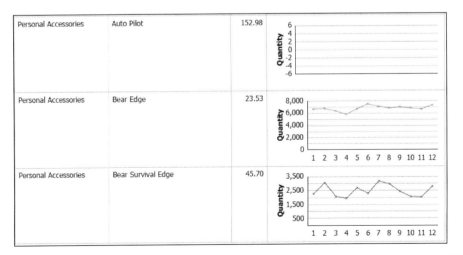

How it works...

Cognos Report Studio allows one report object to be nested within another list report. In the previous recipe of creating sections, we saw that the Report Studio automatically creates nesting for us. In this recipe, we manually created nesting for finer controls.

Master Detail relationship

We need to define this relationship in the following cases:

1. When outer and inner report objects use different queries.
2. For any nesting other than 'List within List'.

In order to generate the report, Cognos first fires the Master query on the database to retrieve the records. Then for each record, it fires the Detail query with the filtering as defined in Master-Detail relationship.

Hence, the Detail query is executed multiple times, each time with different filtering.

As it has to retrieve very small amount of information at a time, a page of output is returned very quickly. This is particularly useful when the report is accessed interactively.

There's more...

By using separate queries for the outer and inner report object in nesting, we can have more control on what information is retrieved. In this example, we want to show a sales trend (chart) only for one year—we hard coded it to 2004. Hence, the chart query needs to be filtered on year.

However, the outer query (list of product lines and products) does not need this filtering.

As you can see in the report output, there are some rows with no corresponding graph. For example, **Personal Accessories | Auto Pilot**. This means there was no selling of this product in the year 2004. If we had used the same query for the list and the chart, this row would have been filtered out resulting in loss of information (Product name and Unit cost) to the users.

See also

With version 8.4 of Cognos Report Studio, a new feature called 'Microchart' is introduced. This type of chart is particularly useful for such in-line spark chart kind of representation.

This version also allows you to quickly insert a chart within a crosstab by right-clicking on row titles (not one-click action for a list report though).

I would highly recommend exploring and experimenting around these features.

Writing back to the database

This is perhaps the most frequently requested functionality by business users—writing some notes or comments back to database, for a particular entry on the report. Though there is no direct functionality provided in Cognos Report Studio for this, it is still possible to achieve it by putting together multiple tools. This recipe will show you how to do that.

The business wants to see sales figures by products. They want to then write some comments for the products from the same interface. The comments need to be stored in database for future retrieval and updating.

You would need access on the backend database and Framework Manager for this recipe.

 As we are only concentrating on Report Studio in this book, we will not cover the Framework Manager options in depth. The power users and Report Studio developers need not be masters in Framework Modelling, but they are expected to have sufficient knowledge of how it works. There is often a Framework Manager Specialist or modeller in the team who controls the overall schema, implements the business rules, and defines hierarchies in the model.

Getting ready

Create a simple list report with Product key, Product name, and Sales quantity columns. Create appropriate sorting, aggregations, and prompts.

How to do it...

1. We will start by creating a table in the database to store the comments entered by users. For that, open your database client and create a table similar to the one shown here.

   In this recipe, I am using a simple table created in a MS SQL Server 2008 database using the SQL Server Management Studio. The table is defined as follows:

```
CREATE TABLE [gosalesdw].[ProductComments](

     [ProductID] [int] NOT NULL,

     [Comment] [varchar](255) NULL,

  CONSTRAINT [PK_ProductComments] PRIMARY KEY CLUSTERED

  (

     [ProductID] ASC
```

```
)WITH (PAD_INDEX  = OFF, STATISTICS_NORECOMPUTE  = OFF, IGNORE_
DUP_KEY = OFF, ALLOW_ROW_LOCKS  = ON, ALLOW_PAGE_LOCKS  = ON) ON
[PRIMARY]

) ON [PRIMARY]
```

2. After creating the above table in the backend, we will now write a *stored procedure* that will accept **Product Key** and **Comments**. It will enter this information in the table and then return all the Product Keys and corresponding Comments back.

```
CREATE PROCEDURE [dbo].[InsertComment] @ProductID int, @Comments
VARCHAR(255)
AS
BEGIN
IF ((select count(*) from
gosalesdw.ProductComments
where ProductID = @ProductID) = 0)
INSERT INTO gosalesdw.ProductComments VALUES (@ProductID,@
Comments)
ELSE
UPDATE gosalesdw.ProductComments
SET Comment = @Comments WHERE ProductID = @ProductID
END
Select ProductID,Comment from gosalesdw.ProductComments
GO
```

3. Please ensure that the user account used to access the database from Cognos, has been given EXECUTE permission on above Stored Procedure. On SQL Server, you can do that using GRANT PERMISSION command.

4. Now open your Framework Model and import this Stored Procedure as a **Stored Proc Query Subject**. You need to configure the input parameters as *Prompts*. This is shown in the following screenshot:

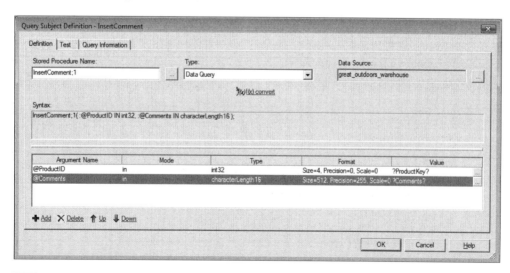

As you can see in the picture, **@ProductID** and **@Comments** are the Stored Procedure parameters. They have 'in' mode which means they accept input. For their value, we are defining prompts as **?ProductKey?** and **?Comments?** respectively.

5. Verify the model and publish it.

6. Now, we will create a new report which users will use to insert the **Comments** about product. For that start with a new list report.

7. Use the **InsertComment** stored proc Query Subject for this report. Drag **Product ID** and **Comment** columns on this report.

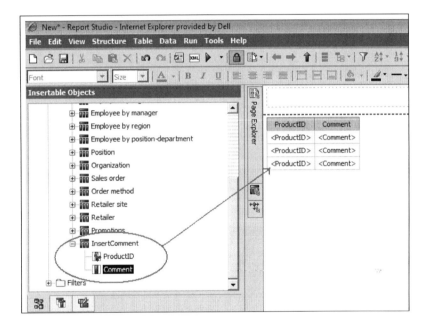

8. Create a prompt page for this report. Insert a **Text Value** type of prompt and connect it to the existing parameter called **Comment**.

9. Save this report as drill report. We will call it as '2.5 Writing Back to Database – Drill' in this recipe.

10. Now re-open the first report. Drag a **Text Item** as a new column on the report and define text as **Insert Comment**.

Product key	Product name	Quantity	Write-Back to Database
<Product key>	<Product name>	<Quantity>	Insert Comment
<Product key>	<Product name>	<Quantity>	Insert Comment
<Product key>	<Product name>	<Quantity>	Insert Comment

11. Create a drill-through from this text column by clicking on the drill-through icon. Set '2.5 Writing Back to Database – Drill' as drill target. Check the option of **Open in New Window**.

12. Edit the parameter for this drill by clicking the edit button.

13. Map the **ProductKey** parameter to the **Product key** data item.

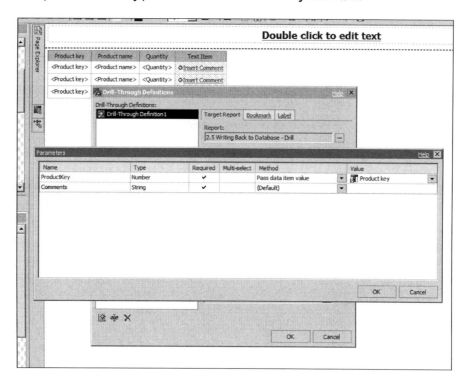

14. Run the report to test it.

How it works...

Cognos Report Studio on its own cannot perform data manipulation on a database. It cannot fire DML statements and hence can't write back to database.

However, Cognos allows reports to execute the Stored Procedures and show the result output on report page. For this, we need to import the Stored Procedure as Query Subject within Framework Manager. When a report that uses this query subject is run, Cognos executes the Stored Proc on database. We can use this opportunity to perform some DML operations, for example, inserting or updating rows in tables.

When we import a Stored Proc into Framework Model, it allows us to define an expression for every input parameter. In step 3 of this recipe, we defined the parameter value to be prompts. The prompt parameters, namely **ProductKey** and **Comments** then become visible in the report.

Once we have imported the Stored Proc in Framework Model, mapped the input parameter to prompts and published package, we are ready to start with reports.

We created a report (drill report) to use the stored proc and hence allow users to insert the comments. In this report, we created a text prompt and linked it to 'Comments' parameter. The Product Key is passed from main report. This way we achieve the write-back to the database.

After inserting/updating the row, Stored Proc returns all the records from the comments table. We show those records in a simple list report to users.

There's more...

This recipe is a very basic example to demonstrate the capability. You can build upon this idea and perform more sophisticated operations on database.

Adding conditional formatting

The business wants to see company sales figure by years and quarters. They want to highlight the entries where sales are below 5,000,000.

We will assume that database provides us the 'Quarter number' and we need to convert that to words. We will use conditional formatting for that. Also, where sales is below 5 million, the cell will be shown in red using another conditional variable.

Getting ready

Create a simple list report with **Current year** and **Current quarter** columns from the **Sales | Time Dimension** query subject.

Drag **Quantity** from **Sales Fact**.

Group by current year and sort by current quarter.

How to do it...

1. Go to **Condition Explorer** and click on **Variables**.

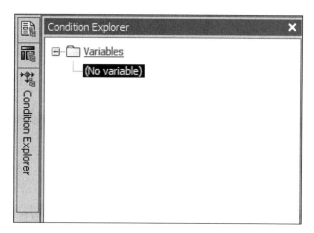

2. Drag a new string variable from **Insertable Objects** pane. Define the expression as: [Query1].[Current quarter].

3. Change the name of variable to Convert_to_words.

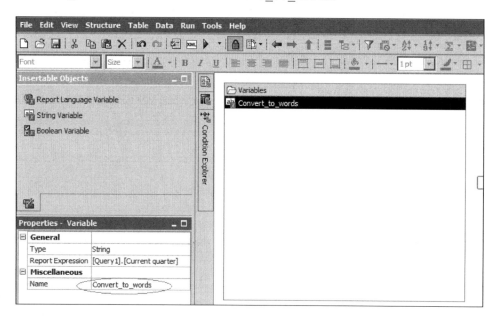

4. Add four values for the variable; the numbers 1 to 4.

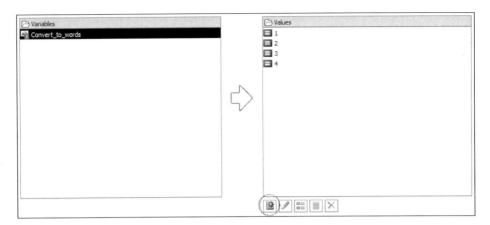

5. Now add a Boolean variable and define it as:
    `[Query1].[Quantity]<5000000`.

6. Call this variable as `Show_Red`.

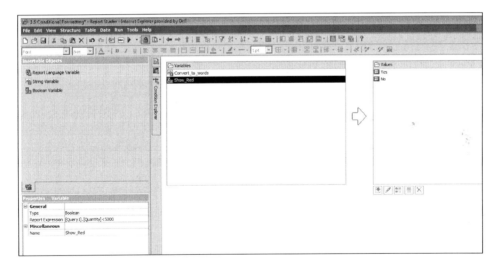

7. Go to report page and select the **Current quarter** column. For **Text source variable** property, select `Convert_to_words` as the variable.

8. Select **Quantity** columns and attach `Show_Red` to the **Style Variable** property.

9. Now from **Conditional Explorer**, iterate through every condition. For the different values of `Convert_to_words` and set corresponding text for the Current quarter column, that is, set to **First Quarter** for value 1, and so on.

10. For `Show_Red` as yes, select **Quantity** column and change the background color to red.

11. Run the report to test the output.

Current year	Current quarter	Quantity
2004	First Quarter	4,877,058
	Second Quarter	5,105,718
	Third Quarter	5,110,315
	Fourth Quarter	5,081,639
2005	First Quarter	6,258,427
	Second Quarter	5,579,643
	Third Quarter	5,556,853
	Fourth Quarter	6,129,762
2006	First Quarter	6,094,787
	Second Quarter	6,783,135
	Third Quarter	6,467,989
	Fourth Quarter	6,595,879
2007	First Quarter	8,382,882
	Second Quarter	8,344,594
	Third Quarter	2,868,410

How it works...

Here we are defining 'Conditional variables' to trap the specific conditions and perform required action on corresponding rows. There are three types of conditional variables: String, Boolean, and Report language variable.

String variable

This type of variable allows you to define different possible values that the expression can be evaluated into. You only need to define the values for which you need to define specific style or text. The rest are taken care of by the 'Other' condition.

Boolean variable

This variable is useful when the expression only evaluates into true or false and you need to format the entries accordingly.

Report language variable

This type of variable returns the language in which report is run by the user. You don't need to define any expression for this type of variable. You simply need to choose the languages for which you want to perform certain actions (like display titles in corresponding language, or show the respective country flag in header).

Here, we have used one variable of String type and one of Boolean type.

There's more...

Style variable property

By assigning a variable to this property, we can control the styling aspect of the object which includes font, colors, data format, visibility, and so on.

Text source variable property

By assigning a variable to this property, we can control the text/values being shown for that object. We can provide static text or a report expression. We can also choose to show value or label of another data item in the selected object.

In this example, we used this property to display the appropriate quarter name. Please note that it was possible to achieve the same result by putting a CASE statement in the data expression. However, the purpose here is to highlight the function of text source variable.

Running difference: Negative values in brackets and red

Business owners need to see the sales figures by months and their month-on-month difference.

If the difference is negative (fall in sales) then it needs to be shown in red and values need to be in brackets.

Getting ready

Create a simple list report with **Time Dimension | Current year**, **Time Dimension | Current month**, and **Sales fact | Quantity** as columns.

Group **Current** year and sort **Current month** ascending.

How to do it...

1. Add a new query calculation to the list. Define the expression as:

   ```
   running-difference([Quantity])
   ```

   Call this item as "Running Difference".

2. Open the **Data Format** properties for this calculation from **Property** list.

3. Set the **Format type** as **Number** and the **Negative Sign Symbol** as brackets **()**.

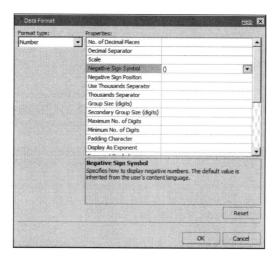

4. Now go to **Condition Explorer** and create a new condition variable of Boolean type. Define the condition as:

```
[Query1].[Running Difference] < 0
```

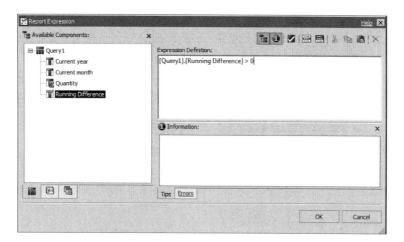

5. Call the variable as `Show_Red`.

6. Now go back to report page and select the **Running Difference** column. Assign `Show_Red` variable as **Style Variable** from the property list.

7. Choose the **Yes** condition for `Show_Red` from the conditional explorer. Select 'Running Difference' column from the list and open its Font properties.

8. Set the font foreground color to red.

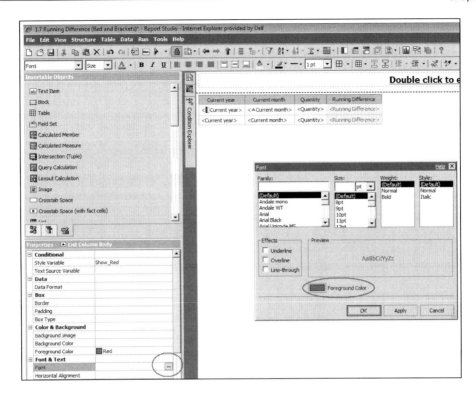

9. Click the **OK** button. Double click on the green bar to come out of condition. Run the report to test.

Current year	Current month	Quantity	Running Difference
2004	1	1,604,216	
	2	1,607,491	3,275
	3	1,665,351	57,860
	4	1,542,002	(123,349)
	5	1,704,903	162,901
	6	1,858,813	153,910
	7	1,750,683	(108,130)
	8	1,719,957	(30,726)
	9	1,639,675	(80,282)
	10	1,554,362	(85,313)
	11	1,689,478	135,116
	12	1,837,799	148,321
2005	1	2,047,167	209,368
	2	2,227,565	180,398
	3	1,983,695	(243,870)
	4	1,917,087	(66,608)
	5	1,800,216	(116,871)
	6	1,862,340	62,124
	7	1,763,284	(99,056)
	8	1,825,241	61,957

How it works...

Running difference

One purpose of this recipe is to introduce you to powerful aggregation functions provided by Cognos. The **Running difference** function returns difference between value in current row and previous row. You can also control the scope and level of aggregation.

In this example, we leave the scope and level of aggregation to default.

There are other such functions provided in Report Studio (for example, Running-maximum, Running-Count, Running-Total, and so on) which are useful in real life scenarios.

Showing negative values in red and brackets

MS Excel has traditionally been the most popular and widely-used tool for information access. It is easy to use and gives enough power for the business users to do their analysis. It readily allows you to display negative numbers in red and brackets, which is a popular choice in the finance world.

However, under the Data Format options of Report Studio, you can only choose to display the negative numbers in brackets. You cannot specify to show them in different colors. Hence, we have to create a conditional variable here and define the foreground color accordingly.

There was this big limitation in Report Studio up to version 8.2. Imagine that you have 15 numerical measures to be formatted in a similar way. In such case, you need to create 15 conditional variables and assign them to each column. This problem is solved with a new feature introduced in version 8.3 onwards. Please refer to the next recipe for this.

New conditional styling with v8.3 onwards

In this recipe, you will learn about the new conditional styles property introduced in Report Studio which, in my humble opinion, is the best feature added to make a report author's life less tedious.

Assume that the following report needs to be formatted such that quantities below 1.7M will be highlighted with red background and those above 2M should be green. Also, we need the negative values for Running Difference (month-on-month) to be shown in red and in a bracket.

Current year	Current month	Quantity	Running Difference
< Current year >	< ▲ Current month >	<Quantity>	<Running Difference>
<Current year >	<Current month >	<Quantity>	<Running Difference>

As shown in previous recipe, this would have needed us to define two conditional variables.

Then attach each to the corresponding column as 'Style variable' to define the styles. With one more such numeric column, the author had to define one more variable and repeat the exercise. Let's see how the new conditional styling feature solves this problem.

Getting ready

Write a new report similar to the one shown in the previous screenshot. Use Report Studio version 8.3 or later.

How to do it...

1. Select the **Quantity** column on report page.

2. Open the new **Conditional Styles** dialog from **Properties** pane.

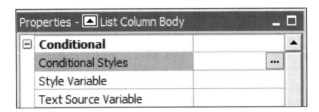

Alternatively, you can also click on the **Conditional Styles** button 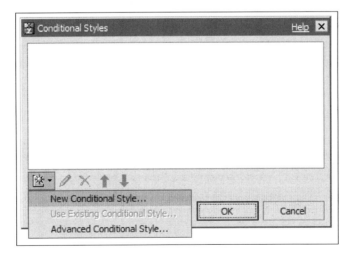 from the toolbar.

3. Create a **New Conditional Style**.

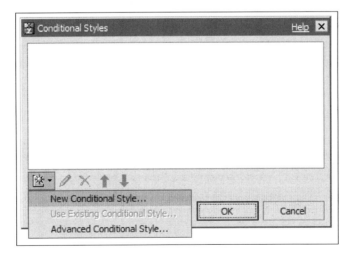

4. Choose quantity to base the conditions on.

5. Define three values (0, 1.7 million and 2 million) by hitting the new value button on bottom left corner. This will look like the following:

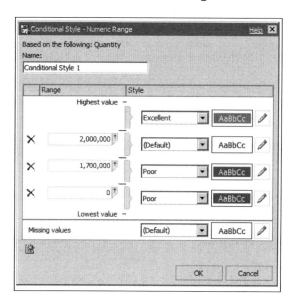

Also choose corresponding styles for each range as shown in the screenshot. Give appropriate name, like **Quantity colors** in this case.

6. Similarly, define the negative values for **Running Difference** column to be shown in red.

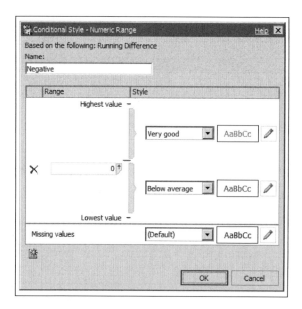

7. Run the report to test it.

Current year	Current month	Quantity	Running Difference
2004	1	1,604,216	
	2	1,607,491	3,275
	3	1,665,351	57,860
	4	1,542,002	(123,349)
	5	1,704,903	162,901
	6	1,858,813	153,910
	7	1,750,683	(108,130)
	8	1,719,957	(30,726)
	9	1,639,675	(80,282)
	10	1,554,362	(85,313)
	11	1,689,478	135,116
	12	1,837,799	148,321
2005	1	2,047,167	209,368
	2	2,227,565	180,398

How it works...

With this new feature, we can now define styling for any column without explicitly defining the conditional variable. The styling can be based on the values on the column itself (8.3 onwards) or some other column (8.4 onwards).

Also, defining actual formatting (font, color, border, and so on) for different conditions is now done within one dialog box. This is more author-friendly than traversing through the conditional variable pane and choosing each condition.

There's more...

The previous example defines very basic value-based range or classification.

You can also choose 'Advanced Conditional Style' option under this property, which allows you to define an expression and have better control over conditions than just classifying the values into ranges.

Conditional block: Many reports in one

The purpose of this recipe is to introduce you to a very useful and powerful control of Report Studio called **Conditional block**.

Users want a report on sales figures. They want the facility to split the numbers by product lines, periods, or retailer region, any one at a time. For convenience purposes, they don't want three different reports, instead they are looking for one report with the facility to choose between the report types.

Getting ready

Create a report with three list objects. Define the list columns as follows:

> ▸ **List 1**: **Product | Product lines** and **Sales fact | Quantity**.

> ▸ **List 2** :**Time dimension | Current year**, **Time dimension | Current month** and **Sales fact | Quantity**.

> ▸ **List 3**: **Retailer site | Region** and **Sales fact | Quantity**.

Define appropriate grouping, sorting, and aggregation for all the list objects. Make sure that all objects use different queries.

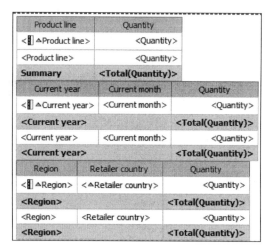

How to do it...

1. We will start by creating a prompt for report type. Go to **Page Explorer** and add a prompt page.

2. Drag a new value prompt object on the prompt page. Define parameter name as **paramReportType**. Do not define any filtering, use value, or display value in the prompt wizard.

3. Select the value prompt and open **Static Choices** from its properties.

4. Define three static choices as shown in the following screenshot:

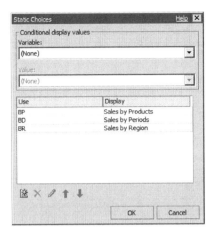

5. Now go to **Condition Explorer** and create a new String Variable. Define it as:
   `ParamValue('paramReportType')`.

6. Add three values for this variable as: BD, BP, and BR. Change the name of the variable to `ReportType`.

7. Now go to the report page. Add a new **Conditional block** from the 'Insertable Objects' pane.

8. Select the conditional block and open the **Block Variable** dialog from the properties. Select `ReportType` variable from the dropdown and then click the **OK** button.

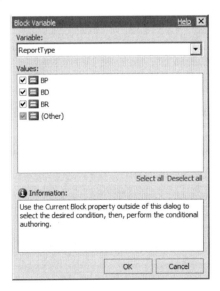

9. Now choose **BP** as the current block from properties. Select the first list object that shows sales quantity by products. Drag this list into the conditional block. (Please note that you need to use the Ancestor button to select the whole list before dragging in).

10. Change the current block property of the conditional block to BD. Drag the 'Sales by Periods' list into the block.

11. Repeat the same for BR and the last list object.

12. On the Report Page header, select the **Double click to edit text** item. Change its **Source type** property to **Report** expression.

13. Define the expression as `ParamDisplayValue('paramReportType')`.

14. Run the report to test it.

How it works...

We saw how to define conditional variables and use them as style variables in the 'Conditional formatting' recipe. In this recipe, we are checking how conditional variables can be used with the conditional blocks.

A conditional block is a useful component that allows you to show certain objects in a certain condition. While condition styling and rendering are for finer control, conditional blocks are useful for coarse actions like showing/hiding whole object and switching between objects.

Here, all list objects use different queries. So, each query subject will have only the required columns. Depending on the prompt selection, only one of those queries will be fired and will bring back appropriate columns.

It was possible to have just one list object and one query subject with all columns, and hide/show columns are required. This will be done using conditional styling that you already learnt. However, the purpose of this recipe is to introduce you to conditional blocks. Now you can be creative and use the conditional blocks in real life scenarios. One such example can be, showing a 'No data' message when query returns no rows.

Please note that we checked for the 'Use value' in condition variable (`paramValue`) whereas we showed the 'Display value' (`paramDisplayValue`) in header. This topic was discussed in *Chapter 1*.

There's more...

It is good practice to define something to be displayed for the 'Other' condition of the conditional variable. Do not keep the block empty for any condition, unless that is the requirement.

Conditional block finds its application in many scenarios. For example, showing certain warnings like 'No records found' or displaying summary or detailed report depending on the user's choice.

Drill-through from crosstab intersection

We have a crosstab report that shows sales quantity by month and order method. We need to create drill-through links from months and sales values.

Getting ready

Create two target reports for the drill-throughs. One takes only **Month** as parameter. The other takes **Month** and **Order Method** (Henceforth referred to as Drill-1 and Drill-2 reports respectively).

Create a simple crosstab report to be used as main report. Pull **Time dimension | Month** on rows, **Order method | Order method** on columns, and **Sales fact | Quantity** as measure.

How to do it...

1. Select the **Month** item placed on crosstab rows. Click on the drill-through definition button ![icon] from the toolbar.

2. This opens the drill-through definitions dialog. Create a new definition. Select Drill-1 as **Target Report**. Map the month parameter with the month data item.

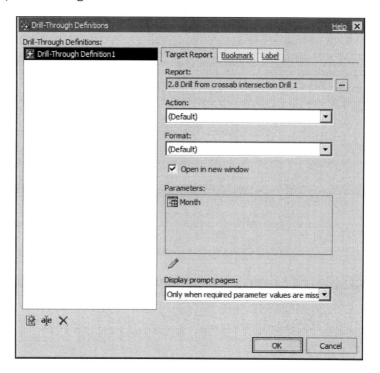

3.   Now click on the unlock button from toolbar to unlock the items.
4.   Select the text item from crosstab intersection. Hit the drill-through button again.
5.   Create a drill link to Drill-2.
6.   Run the report and test both the drill links.

How it works...

You will notice that when we created the drill-through from row titles (month), we didn't have to unlock the items. Whereas, for the intersection, we had to unlock them.

Now try one thing. Lock the report objects again and select the crosstab intersection. Try to create drill-through now. You will see that the drill-through definition button is disabled.

For some unknown reason, Report Studio doesn't allow you to create drill-through from crosstab intersection. You need to select the 'Fact cells' class or the 'Text item' within the intersection. By unlocking the object, we select the text item within the intersection and create a link from there.

Another way is to right-click on the intersection, and to choose 'Select Fact cells'. This will enable the drill-through button and let you define one.

Overriding crosstab intersection drill-through definition

Let us consider an extension of the last recipe. Let us say the users want to see a *Discontinuous crosstab* as main report. Instead of just **Order methods** on column, we need to display **Order methods** and **Product lines** as columns.

The rows display **Month**. Measure is sales quantity.

The drill-through from the intersection has to go to the appropriate report depending on whether the column is **Product line** or **Order method**.

Getting ready

Create a new drill-through target that accepts **Month** and **Product line** as parameters. We will call it as Drill-3 from now on.

For the main report, we will use the same crosstab report as in the last recipe.

How to do it...

1. We will start by creating the *discontinuous crosstab* on the main report. We already have **Order method** on columns. Drag **Product line** also on the crosstab, as column. The report will look like this.

Quantity	<#Product line#>	<#Order method#>
✛ <#Month#>	✛ <#1234#>	✛ <#1234#>
✛ <#Month#>	✛ <#1234#>	✛ <#1234#>

2. Now select the intersection cells under the product line column.

3. From its Properties, set **Define contents** to **Yes**. This will make the intersection empty.

4. Unlock the report items. Drag **Quantity** from **Data Items** pane again on report, in this empty crosstab intersection.

5. You will notice that there is no drill-through for this instance of **Quantity**.

Quantity	<#Product line#>	<#Order method#>
✛ <#Month#>	<Quantity>	✛ <#1234#>
✛ <#Month#>	<Quantity>	✛ <#1234#>

6. Now select this instance of **Quantity** and define the drill-through definition in the same way as you did previously. The only difference will be that the target report is **Drill-3** which accepts **Product line** and **Month**.

7. Run the report to test both the drill-throughs from intersections.

How it works...

In the last recipe, we saw that creating drill-through link from crosstab intersection needs that we unlock the item and create it from the text item within.

In the case of a discontinuous report, we have different items on columns (product lines and order methods). However, when you select the text item from intersection, Report Studio doesn't distinguish between them.

Hence, we need to select the intersection under one of the column items and set its **Define content** to **Yes**. This means we want to override the contents of this intersection and define the contents ourselves.

After changing the property, Report Studio makes that intersection empty. We can then unlock the items and drag any measure/calculation in it. We chose to drag **Quantity** again. Now Report Studio will distinguish between both the **Quantity** items (the one under **Product line** and the one under **Order methods**).

Finally, we defined drill-through to Drill-3 appropriately.

There's more...

You can use the **Define content** option also to override the information being displayed. For example, if you want to show "Revenue" under Product lines instead of showing Quantity.

This also gives you the opportunity to differently define styles and conditional styling.

3
Tips and Tricks: JavaScripts

In this chapter, we will cover the following:

- ▶ Dynamic default values for prompt
- ▶ Change title of value of a prompt
- ▶ Applying deselect all on re-runs
- ▶ Textbox validation
- ▶ Showing/Hiding controls dynamically
- ▶ Auto-submitting values
- ▶ Manipulating the date time control
- ▶ Variable width bar charts using JavaScript

Introduction

Report Studio is a web-based tool and the reports designed in Cognos Report Studio are accessed through a web browser. This allows us to do certain web page specific things; for example, embedding our own HTML code or JavaScripts.

Often, business users need certain functionality which is not naturally available in Cognos Report Studio. Hence, a new area has evolved over the period in the Cognos Report Studio developer's world—that is Javascripting.

With JavaScript, we can do certain manipulations on the objects used for prompt pages. Please note that this was not officially introduced in initial Cognos documentation. However, lately many such techniques were published on the Cognos website itself.

In this chapter, we will see some recipes that will teach you very useful and commonly required functionalities achieved using JavaScripts. All these recipes are valid for Cognos versions 8.3 and 8.4. These versions are quite recent and most organisations will be moving on to 8.3/8.4 this year. Also there isn't much material available for these versions on the Internet. Hence, I am providing you with code for these versions.

For prior versions, some code changes will be required. There are a lot of examples and reading material available for prior versions (CRN, 8.1 and 8.2) on the Internet.

After trying these recipes, you can build upon the ideas to write more sophisticated scripts and do a lot with your Cognos Reports. Please note that IBM doesn't directly support these techniques and does not guarantee any upward or backward compatibility. However, they are aware that developers are widely using them, and hence IBM will try to maintain most of the objects, properties, and events in future. (Reference: `http://www-01.ibm.com/support/docview.wss?rs=0&uid=swg24021973`)

The level of JavaScript that we will be using in this chapter is basic. However, if you have never used JavaScript before, I would recommend getting familiar with JavaScript basics using books or online tutorials. http://www.w3schools.com/js is a good resource with a nice collection of samples and provides a quick tool to try your own scripts.

Please note that all the JavaScript-based recipes will need you to enable JavaScript in your web browser. Usually, it is enabled by default.

Dynamic default value for prompt

There is a report which allows users to select a shipment month. The Shipment Month dimension has values up to current month. However, users frequently select prior month. They want the prompt to have prior month selected by default.

Getting ready

Take any report that filters on Shipment Month Key. Add a value prompt to the Shipment Month Key on the prompt page.

How to do it...

1. Select the value prompt and define its sorting such that the Shipment Month Keys are populated in *descending* order.

2. Now, as we know the dimension is always populated up to the current month and values are sorted in descending order, we will write a code that selects second value from top by default.

3. For that, add an **HTML Item** just before the Shipment Month value prompt. Define the HTML as: `<span id = 'A1'>`

4. Add another HTML item just after the value prompt and define it as: `</span>`

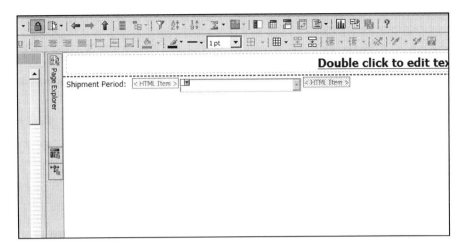

5. Now add another HTML item to the prompt page footer, just after the **Finish** button.

6. Define it as:

```
<script>
var theSpan = document.getElementById("A1");
var a = theSpan.getElementsByTagName("select");   /* This stmt
return an array of all value prompts within span */
for( var i = a.length-1; i >= 0; i-- )   /* now loop through the
elements */
{        var prompts = a[i];
if( prompts.id.match(/PRMT_SV_/))
    {        prompts.selectedIndex = 3;   } /* This selects the second
options from top */
canSubmitPrompt();
}
</script>
```

7. Execute the report to test it.

How it works...

The logic used here is that we first sort the months in descending order and then select the second option from top. As the values populated from the database are up to the latest month, the second value from top will be the previous month.

As mentioned at the beginning of the chapter, Report Studio prompt pages are similar to any other HTML pages with most of the controls being standard web controls. The HTML item in Report Studio is a powerful component which allows us to embed our own code within the page generated by Cognos.

When we put a JavaScript within an HTML item, it is automatically executed when the page loads.

SPAN

With Cognos 8.3, the report viewer architecture has been majorly changed. With CRN 8.1 and 8.2, it was a common practice to define a NAME or ID for the prompt controls and use that to manipulate controls at runtime through JavaScript.

However, version 8.3 onwards, the IDs of the controls are generated randomly and are not fixed. So, it is a little difficult to get hold of a control. For this reason, we have defined a **SPAN** around the control that we want to manipulate.

By wrapping the control within SPAN tags, we will reduce the scope of our search in JavaScript.

GetElementsByTagName

As we want to capture the Value Prompt within span, we search elements with `select` tag within the span A1.

If we want to perform same operation on multiple value prompts, we can put them all within same span. The `GetElementsByTagName` function returns an array of elements with the specified tag.

SelectedIndex

Once a value prompt object is captured in a variable, we can set its `SelectedIndex` property to set the selection to required value.

CanSubmitPrompt

In prior versions, we used the `CheckData()` function to submit the prompt value. This means Report Studio will accept the value and adornments will disappear. However, 8.3 onwards, we can use a global `CanSubmitPrompt()` function for the same purpose.

There's more...

A more suitable example of 'dynamic selection' will be iterating through the value prompt options and selecting one based on a condition.

You can use the Java functions to capture system date and accordingly work out the *Prior Month*. Then traverse through all the values and select an appropriate one. Similarly, you can iterate through all the prompt values and select the required entry based on value instead of hard-coding the `selectedIndex` to 3.

Please refer to one such example on the IBM website at this URL: `http://www-01.ibm.com/support/docview.wss?uid=swg21343424`

Changing title of the dropdown box

In the previous example, the fist line of value prompt shows the data item name, that is, **Month key (Shipment date)**.

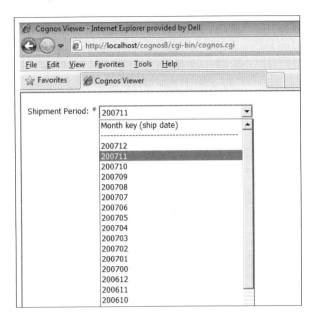

The business wants to change this to a more generic and user-friendly text.

Getting ready

We will use the report generated in the previous recipe.

How to do it...

1. We need to add a line to the JavaScript from the previous recipe to change the text of first option (index 0). For that, open the prompt page of the report created in the previous recipe.

2. Double-click on the HTML item in the prompt footer.

3. Replace the code with the following:

```
<script>
var theSpan = document.getElementById("A1");
var a = theSpan.getElementsByTagName("select");
for( var i = a.length-1; i >= 0; i-- )
{ var prompts = a[i];
```

```
if( prompts.id.match(/PRMT_SV_/))
{       prompts.selectedIndex = 3;
   prompts.options[0].text = 'Choose Shipment Month'; /* This is
the new line added to script */
}
canSubmitPrompt();
}
</script>
```

4. Run the report to test it.

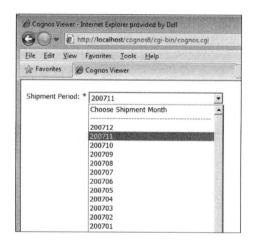

How it works...

By default, the first line of a value prompt is the name of the **data item**.If you define the data item expression within brackets, that is, ([Sales (query)].[Time (ship date)].
[Month key (ship date)]) in this example, then the first line of value prompt is populated by the parameter name.

However, there is no property within Report Studio that would allow us to put a custom title. Hence, we are using JavaScript. We already know how to capture the prompt control using GetElementsbyTagName function. Once it is captured, we can manipulate the values. We change the text property of options[0] element to update the first line of prompt.

There's more...

You can also use the REMOVE() function to remove particular lines of a value prompt. It is often useful to remove the first two lines (title and separator) using the following statements:

```
Prompts.remove(0);
Prompts.remove(1);
Prompts.removeAttribute("hasLabel");
```

Listbox: Applying Deselect All on rerun

There is a report where users can select multiple product lines from a listbox. When they rerun the report, the previous selection is remembered.

Users want the selection to be automatically cleared on re-run.

Getting ready

Select any existing report or create a new sample report that filters on **Product Lines**. Create a **Listbox** type of prompt for the product line. Set its multi-select property to Yes.

How to do it...

1. Wrap the listbox in a span similar to previous recipes; that is, create two HTML items around the listbox and define span A1.

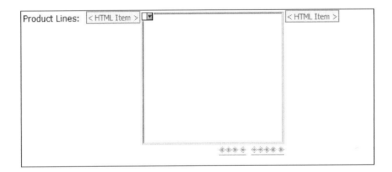

2. Now define a new HTML item in prompt page footer as follows:

```
<script>
var theSpan = document.getElementById("A1");
var a = theSpan.getElementsByTagName("A");
for( var i = a.length-1; i >= 0; i-- )
{ var link = a[i];
if( typeof(link.id) == "string" && link.id.match(/PRMT_(SV|LIST)_
LINK_DESELECT_/) )
{link.fireEvent("onclick");}
}
</script>
```

3. Run the report for any product line. Then re-run the report by clicking the **Run** ▷ button. Notice that the previous prompt selection is cleared.

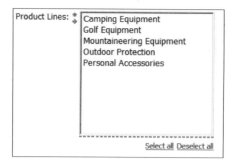

How it works...

With a multi-select listbox control, Report studio throws in two links on the prompt page. These are for SELECT ALL and DESELECT ALL functionalities.

Here we are capturing the **Deselect all** link and then calling it by fireevent() function.

There's more...

You can optionally check for PRMT_(SV|LIST)_LIST_SELECT in the Id and call the **Select All** link when appropriate.

Also, you can use the following line in script if you want to remove a link from the page at run time:

```
link.parentNode.removeChild(link)
```

Validating textbox prompts

There is a report with a textbox prompt. Users are expected to enter a phone number in *(nnn) nnn-nnnn* format in that prompt.

In this recipe, we will write a code to validate the value entered by the user and submit the report only if the value entered is in specified format.

Getting ready

Pick any report and add a textbox prompt to it. We will add a JavaScript to validate that textbox.

How to do it...

1. Wrap the textbox prompt within a SPAN in the same way as we did in prior recipes.

2. Add the following script to the page footer:

```
<script>
function ValidatePage()
{
var theSpan = document.getElementById("A1");
var a = theSpan.getElementsByTagName("input"); /* this captures
the textbox */
for( var i = a.length-1; i >= 0; i-- )
{
var link = a[i];
if( link.id.match(/PRMT_TB_/))
        {phoneRegex = /^\(\d{3}\) \d{3}-\d{4}$/; /* This is
regular expression to allow only the strings in (nnn) nnn-nnnn
format */
        if( !link.value.match( phoneRegex ) ) {
        alert( 'Please enter phone number in (nnn)nnn-nnnn
format' );
        link.focus();
        link.select();
        return; }
    else {promptButtonFinish();}
        }
}
}
/* Below is standard code to get FormWarpRequest*/
var fW = (typeof getFormWarpRequest == "function"
?getFormWarpRequest() : document.forms["formWarpRequest"]);
if ( !fW || fW == undefined) { fW = ( formWarpRequest_THIS_
?formWarpRequest_THIS_ : formWarpRequest_NS_ );}
/* This returns all elements of Button tag */var buttons = fW.getE
lementsByTagName("BUTTON");
for (var i=0; i<buttons.length; i++)
{
        if (buttons[i].id.match(/finish/)) // Capture the finish
button
        {
                if (buttons[i].onclick.toString().
indexOf('finish') > 0)
                { buttons[i].onclick = ValidatePage;} /* This
overrides the FINISH button and attaches it to our function */
        }
}
</script>
```

How it works...

We first define a function called `ValidatePage()` that captures the textbox value and checks whether it follows the required format. We are using the **match** function of JavaScript which allows us to parse the textbox string against our regular expression. The regular expression `^\(\d{3}\) \d{3}-\d{4}$` allows only the string in *(nnn) nnn-nnnn* format. You can read more about regular expressions on the Internet and also try some on this website: `http://www.regular-expressions.info/javascriptexample.html`

If the textbox value matches with our regular expression, we call the `promptButtonFinish()` function to submit the prompt page. Otherwise, we show an error message and set the focus back to the textbox.

Finally, this `ValidatePage()` function is attached to the **Finish** button by second part of the script. We capture the Finish button by its **TagName** ("button") and Id match (`/finish/`), and then override its **OnClick** event.

Show/Hide prompt controls at runtime

A report shows sales quantity by product line and order method. Users need to filter on either product line or order method, any one at the time.

They would like a facility to select which prompt they want to filter on, and depending on the selection, prompt should appear.

Getting ready

Create a list report that shows product lines, order methods, and sales quantity. Create two options filters—one on product lines and the other on order methods.

How to do it...

1. We will start by creating prompts for both the filters. For that, add a prompt page and add two value prompts. Use the prompt wizard to connect them to the parameters (product line and order method).

2. Set the **Hide Adornment** property of both the prompts to **Yes**.

3. Now drag an HTML item just before the product line prompt. Define it as:

```
<Input type = radio Name = r1 title= "Click me to select Product
Line..." Value = "PL" onclick= "radioSelect(this)">Product Line
      
```

```
<Input type = radio Name = r1 title= "Click me to select Order
Method..." Value = "OM" onclick= "radioSelect(this)">Order Method
      
<span id = 'ProductSpan'>
```

4. Now add another HTML item between the product line prompt and order method prompt. Define it as: `</span> <span id = 'OrderSpan'>`.

5. Finally, add a third HTML item after the order method prompt. Define it as:

```
</span>
<script>
var fW = (typeof getFormWarpRequest == "function"
?getFormWarpRequest() : document.forms["formWarpRequest"]);
if ( !fW || fW == undefined) { fW = ( formWarpRequest_THIS_
?formWarpRequest_THIS_ : formWarpRequest_NS_ );}
var theSpan = document.getElementById("ProductSpan");
var a = theSpan.getElementsByTagName('select');
for( var i = a.length-1; i >= 0; i-- )
{ var ProductBox = a[i];
ProductBox.style.display = 'none'; }
theSpan = document.getElementById("OrderSpan");
a = theSpan.getElementsByTagName('select');
for( var i = a.length-1; i >= 0; i-- )
{ var OrderBox = a[i];
OrderBox.style.display = 'none'; }

function radioSelect(rad)
{ if (rad.value == "PL")  /* Hide OrderBox and show ProductBox */
{ ProductBox.style.display = '';
OrderBox.style.display = 'none';
}
else if (rad.value == "OM") /* Hide ProductBox and show OrderBox
*/
{ ProductBox.style.display = 'none';
OrderBox.style.display = '';
}
else /* Hide both controls */
{ ProductBox.style.display = 'none';
OrderBox.style.display = 'none'; }
}
</script>
```

Now your prompt page will look like the following in Report Studio:

Double click to edit text

< HTML Item > | < HTML Item > | < HTML Item >

6. Run the report to test it. You will see two radio buttons. Depending on which one you select, one of the prompts will be visible.

⦿ Product Line   ○ Order Method | Product line   ▾ |

How it works...

Before explaining how this recipe works, I would like the readers to know that it is possible to achieve the required functionality using Conditional Block instead of JavaScript. You would use the auto-submit functionality of radio button prompt, which will then cause the Conditional Block to show appropriate prompt.

If you are using Cognos Report Studio version 8.2 or older, this will refresh the page and will not give a seamless user experience. Hence, you might consider the JavaScript alternative that is explained next. From 8.3 onwards, the whole page is not refreshed. But still you might want to consider JavaScript for a quick response time.

This recipe works in three parts. First, we defined the radio buttons in the HTML item. This is our own code so we can control what happens when users select any of the radio buttons.

Then, we wrapped both the prompts into spans so that we can capture them in the JavaScript and manipulate the properties.

Finally, we wrote the JavaScript to toggle the display of prompts depending on the radio button selection.

There's more...

When the prompt is hidden through the `style.display` property, the adornments aren't hidden. That is why we set the adornments off in step 2.

More Info

When the visibility of a control is turned off, the control is still present on the form and the selected value (if any) is also submitted in the query when user clicks on **Finish** button.

Hence, it is preferred that we reset the selection to `index(0)` when a prompt is hidden. For information on how to select a value through JavaScript, please refer to *Dynamic default value for prompt* recipe of this chapter.

Automatic selection and submission of values

A business report has numerous prompts on the prompt page. Often, users want to run a report for the latest month in the database, 'Camping Equipment' product and 'E-mail' as a order method.

They want a facility to either manually select vales for these prompts; or alternatively, run the report for the above selections on single button click.

In this recipe, we will add a custom button on prompt page that will allow users to quickly run the report for frequently used selections.

Getting ready

Create a list report with product line, order method, and sales quantity as columns.

Create optional filters on product line, order method, and Shipment Month that is, Month Key (Shipment Date).

Create a prompt page with three value prompts for these filters.

How to do it...

1. We will start by wrapping the prompts within spans, so that they can be captured easily in JavaScript. Add one HTML tag before and one after each prompt to define Spans. Define the spans as **PL**, **OM**, and **SM** for **Product Line**, **Order Method**, and **Shipment Month** respectively. This is similar to the wrapping we did in most of the prior recipes.

2. Add one more HTML item on the prompt page after all the prompts, and define it as follows:

```
<script>
function defaultSelect()
{
var a = document.getElementById("PL");
var PL = a.getElementsByTagName("select");
```

```
for( var i = PL.length-1; i >= 0; i-- ) /* Captures Product Line
prompt */
{
var PLBox = PL[i];
}

a = document.getElementById("OM");
var OM = a.getElementsByTagName("select");
for( var i = OM.length-1; i >= 0; i-- ) /* Captures Order Method
prompt */
{
var OMBox = OM[i];
}
a = document.getElementById("SM");
var SM = a.getElementsByTagName("select");
for( var i = SM.length-1; i >= 0; i-- ) /* Captures Shipment Month
prompt */
{
var SMBox = SM[i];
}
PLBox.selectedIndex = 2;
OMBox.selectedIndex = 2;
SMBox.selectedIndex = 2;
canSubmitPrompt();
promptButtonFinish();
}
</script>
<button type="button" onclick="defaultSelect()" class="bt"
style="font-size:8pt">Run for Defaults</button>
```

Now your prompt will look similar to the following screenshot in Report Studio:

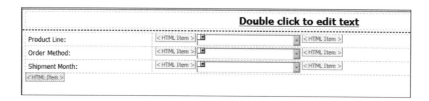

3. Run the report to test it. You should see a button that you did not see in Report Studio. When you click on the button, it will automatically select the prompt values and run the report.

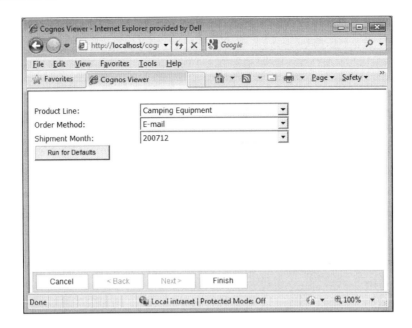

How it works...

In this recipe, we are mixing two techniques learnt from previous recipes. In the *Dynamic default selection* recipe, we learnt how to capture a value prompt and change its selection.

So, we are using the same technique here but instead of calling on Page Load, we are calling the routine when users click on the button.

Then we are also using a function `promptButtonFinish()` that we used in the 'Textbox validation' recipe to submit the prompt.

The custom button is defined using `<button>` tag and as it is our own object, we can easily make it call our JavaScript function for the onclick event.

As mentioned in the 'Dynamic default selection' recipe, practically you will not hard-code the `selectedIndex` in your script. Instead, you should traverse through all prompt selection options and choose one based on the value. For example, look for 'Camping Equipment' so that its order in the list won't matter.

Please refer to one such example on the IBM website at this URL: `http://www-01.ibm.com/support/docview.wss?uid=swg21343424`

There's more...

This technique is very useful in real-life scenarios. You can define multiple buttons for different *frequently used* selections. It saves time for users and makes the reports convenient to use, especially when there are more than five prompts.

Manipulating Date Time control

There is a report that allows users to filter on Shipment Date Time using **Date Time** control. By default, Cognos selects current date and midnight as the date and time.

Report Studio allows you to override this with another static default value. However, business usually runs the report for the end of previous business day (5 PM).

In this recipe, we will learn how to change the default date and time for a Date Time control to the end of the previous business day.

Getting ready

Create a dummy report that shows sales quantity by shipment day. Define filter on shipment day.

How to do it...

1. We will start by adding a date and time control to the report. For that add a new prompt page.

2. From insertable objects, drag **Date & Time Prompt** on the prompt page. Connect it to the **Shipment Day** filter using appropriate parameter in the prompt wizard.

3. Now select the prompt and set its **Name** property to **shipmentDate**.

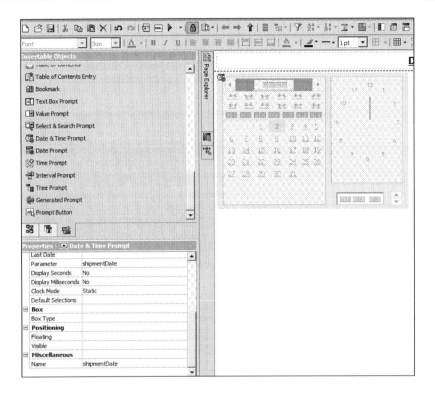

4. Now add an HTML item to the prompt footer after the **Finish** button. Define it as:

```
<script>
function subtractDay ()
{ var dtToday = new Date();
  var dtYesterday = new Date( dtToday - 86400000 );
// NOTE 86400000 = 24 hours * 60 (minutes per hour) * 60 (seconds
per minute) * 1000 milliseconds per second)
var strYesterday = [dtYesterday.getUTCFullYear(), dtYesterday.
getMonth()+1, dtYesterday.getDate()].join("-");
return strYesterday;
}
function subtractTime ()
{ var Time = "17:00:00.000"; return Time;
}
pickerControlshipmentDate.setValue( subtractDay() );
timePickershipmentDate.setValue( subtractTime() );
</script>
```

5. Run the report to test. You will see that the value of the 'Date Time control' is set to previous day, 5 PM by default.

How it works...

Here we use standard JavaScript functions to work out the date of the previous day. Please note that this date is computed based on system date on user's machine.

Then we apply this date to the 'Date & Time control' using a `pickerControl<name>` object. Also we set the time to 5 PM using `setValue` function of `timePicker<name>` object.

You can similarly do more date and string manipulations to find `First of Month`, `Last of Month`, and so on. I found the following script on the Internet for generating commonly used dates.

```JavaScript
<script language="JavaScript" runat="SERVER">
var today = new Date();
var thisYear = today.getYear();
var thisMonth = today.getMonth();
var thisDay = today.getDate();
function rw(s1, s2)
{
Response.Write("<tr><td>"+s1+"</td><td>"+s2+"</td></tr>");
}
Response.Write("<table border='1'>");
rw("Today:", today.toDateString());
//Years
var fdly = new Date(thisYear - 1, 0, 1);
rw("First day of last year:", fdly.toDateString());
var ldly = new Date(thisYear, 0, 0);
rw("Last day of last year:", ldly.toDateString());
var fdty = new Date(thisYear, 0, 1);
rw("First day of this year:", fdty.toDateString());
var ldty = new Date(thisYear + 1, 0, 0);
rw("Last day of this year:", ldty.toDateString());
var fdny = new Date(thisYear + 1, 0 ,1);
rw("First day of next year:", fdny.toDateString());
var ldny = new Date(thisYear + 2, 0, 0);
rw("Last day of next year:", ldny.toDateString());
//Months
var fdlm = new Date(thisYear, thisMonth - 1 ,1);
rw("First day of last month:", fdlm.toDateString());
var ldlm = new Date(thisYear, thisMonth, 0);
rw("Last day of last month:", ldlm.toDateString());
rw("Number of days in last month:", ldlm.getDate());
var fdtm = new Date(thisYear, thisMonth, 1);
rw("First day of this month:", fdtm.toDateString());
var ldtm = new Date(thisYear, thisMonth + 1, 0);
rw("Last day of this month:", ldtm.toDateString());
```

```
rw("Number of days in this month:", ldtm.getDate());
var fdnm = new Date(thisYear, thisMonth + 1, 1);
rw("First day of next month:", fdnm.toDateString());
var ldnm = new Date(thisYear, thisMonth + 2, 0);
rw("Last day of next month:", ldnm.toDateString());
rw("Number of days in next month:", ldnm.getDate());
Response.Write("</table>");
</script>
```

There's more...

You can write more sophisticated functions to work out the previous working day instead of just the previous day.

See also

You can mix this technique with other recipes in this chapter to tie the selection event with button click or radio buttons, that is, a particular date/time can be selected when user clicks on the button or selects a radio button.

Variable width bar chart using JavaScript

A report shows **Unit cost** and **Unit price** of all products. It also works out the **Profit Margin** from these two.

Business owners are naturally more interested in products with a high profit margin as well as a high unit price.

In this recipe, we will create 'Variable width bar chart' using JavaScript, which shows a bar for every product. The length of bar will indicate the Profit Margin, whereas width will indicate the unit price.

Getting ready

Create a simple list report with **Product name**, **Unit cost**, and **Unit price** as columns.

Also add a calculated item, called **Margin**, to the list to compute the Profit Margin and define it as: `([Unit price]-[Unit cost])/[Unit cost]`.

How to do it...

1. Drag a new HTML item on the list report as a new column.

2. Unlock the report objects using Unlock button . Add four more HTML items in the column where you added above HTML item. The report should look like this in the Studio:

Product name	Unit cost	Unit price	Margin	HTML Item
<Product name>	<Unit cost>	<Unit price>	<Margin>	< HTML Item > < HTML Item > < HTML Item > < HTML Item > < HTML Item >
<Product name>	<Unit cost>	<Unit price>	<Margin>	< HTML Item > < HTML Item > < HTML Item > < HTML Item > < HTML Item >
<Product name>	<Unit cost>	<Unit price>	<Margin>	< HTML Item > < HTML Item > < HTML Item > < HTML Item > < HTML Item >

3. Now define the first HTML item as:

```
<script>
var barlen=100*((
```

4. For the second HTML item, set the **Source Type** to **Data Item Value** and select **Margin** as a data item.

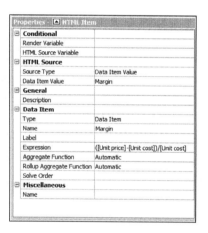

5. Define the third HTML item as:

```
)) ;
var barheight=((
```

6. For the fourth HTML item, again set the **Source Type** to **Data Item Value**. Select **Unit price** as **Data Item**.

7. Define the fifth and last HTML as:

```
)/10) ;
var myBar='<div style="background-color:blue; width:' +barlen+';
height:' + barheight +'"></div>' ;
```

```
document.write(myBar) ;
</script>
```

8. Run the report to see the output. It will look like this:

Product name	Unit cost	Unit price	Margin	HTML Item
Aloe Relief	1.92	5.23	172%	
Astro Pilot	108.55	173.08	59%	
Auto Pilot	152.98	235.00	54%	
Bear Edge	23.53	40.52	72%	
Bear Survival Edge	45.70	92.29	102%	
Bella	37.17	68.22	84%	
Blue Steel Max Putter	89.41	180.63	102%	
Blue Steel Putter	41.20	90.95	121%	
BugShield Extreme	2.42	7.00	189%	
BugShield Lotion	2.33	7.00	200%	
BugShield Lotion Lite	1.88	7.00	272%	
BugShield Natural	1.86	6.00	223%	
BugShield Spray	1.83	6.01	228%	
Calamine Relief	2.83	6.00	112%	
Canyon Mule Carryall	41.18	73.50	78%	
Canyon Mule Climber Backpack	52.50	76.86	46%	
Canyon Mule Cooler	15.27	32.69	114%	
Canyon Mule Extreme Backpack	238.88	460.52	93%	
Canyon Mule Journey Backpack	213.33	370.86	74%	

As you can see, **Bugshield Lotion Lite** has a huge profit margin. Whereas, **Canyon Mule Extreme Backpack** might have a relatively low margin, but its unit price is high and hence it is also an important product for the business.

In short, the area of the bar (width X height) indicates the importance of a product to the business.

How it works...

Report Studio has in-built chart objects which allow you to create sophisticated and detailed charts. However, in this case, we don't have any complex charting requirements.

We just want to highlight the products with high profitability.

The JavaScript used in this recipe has the following structure:

```
<script>
var barlen=100*((length_driver)) ;
var barheight=((width_driver)/10) ;
var myBar='<div style="background-color:blue; width:' +barlen+';
height:' + barheight +'"></div>' ;
document.write(myBar) ;
</script>
```

We have split it into five HTML items so that the `length_driver` and `width_driver` can be replaced with any data item from the query. We have used the **Margin** and **Unit price**, but any other data item or calculation can be used as per the business requirement.

The multiplier (100) and divisor (10) are scaling factors as we need to scale the actual values to pixels. We know that **Margin** is in percentage and the value range is approximately 0.5 to 30. Hence, we multiply it with 100 to get the bars in range of 50 to 300 pixels long. Similarly, **Unit Price** is scaled down by 10 to get bar width in range of 5 to 50 pixels.

You can change the scaling to appropriate values in order to achieve nice looking bars.

There's more...

JavaScripts are executed on the client side within the web browser; hence there is no load on the server to produce these charts.

However, please note that this technique is useful only when users are interactively using the report in web browser. Also, users must have JavaScripts enabled in their browser. It doesn't work for PDFs, Excel, or any output format other than HTML.

4

Tips and Tricks: Report Page

In this chapter, we will cover the following:

- ▶ Showing images dynamically (Traffic light report)
- ▶ Handling missing image issue
- ▶ Dynamic links to external website (Google Map example)
- ▶ Alternating drill link
- ▶ Showing tool tips on reports
- ▶ Achieving minimum column width
- ▶ Merged cells in Excel output
- ▶ Work sheet name in Excel output
- ▶ Changing column titles conditionally

Introduction

In this chapter, I will show you some tricks that I have learnt over the period. As mentioned before in this book, though Cognos Report Studio has some limitations, it does have a flexible structure which allows us to implement some workarounds and overcome the limitations.

Showing images dynamically (Traffic Light report)

In first chapter, we created a report under the 'Running Difference' recipe. This report shows the *month-on-month* difference in sales quantity.

Business wants to give this report a 'dashboard' look by putting Traffic Light images (red, yellow, and green) in each row, based on whether there is rise in sales or fall.

Getting ready

We will use the "Running Difference: negative values in brackets and red" report based on the recipe in Chapter 2 for this.

Open that report in Cognos Report Studio and save a copy with a new name.

 Please note that you will need administrator rights on the Cognos server to complete this recipe. If the server is installed on your personal machine, you will have these rights by default.

1. For this recipe, we need to first create three icons or images for red, yellow, and green. They should be already available on the Cognos server under `{Cognos Installation}\webcontent\samples\images` folder. If not, then create them using any image editor software or use the images supplied with this book

2. Once you have the three images which you need to conditionally show on the report, place them on the Cognos server under `{Cognos Installation}\webcontent\samples\images` folder. (If the folder is not there, create one).

3. Change the IIS security to allow 'Anonymous Read and Browse' accesses.

4. Now open the report that shows the month-on-month running differences.

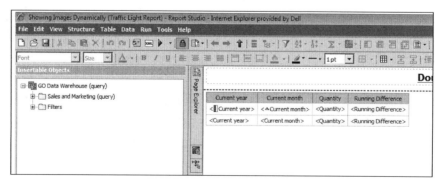

5. Insert a new 'image' from the insertable objects pane on the list report, as a new column.

6. Now go to **Condition Explorer** and create a new string variable. Define the expression as:

```
if ([Query1].[Running Difference] > 0)
then ('green')
else if ([Query1].[Running Difference] < 0)
then ('red')
else ('yellow')
```

7. Call this variable **Traffic** and define three possible values for the same (red, yellow, and green).

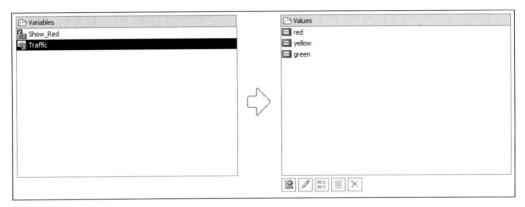

8. Now go back to the report page. Select the image. Open its **URL Source Variable** dialog. Choose the variable **Traffic** and click **OK**.

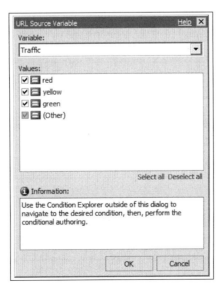

9. From Condition Explorer, choose 'red' condition. Now click on the image again. It will allow you to define the image URL for this condition.

10. Set the URL to: `../samples/images/Red.jpg`

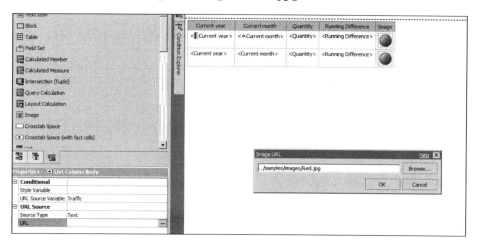

11. Similarly, define the URL for 'yellow' and 'green' conditions as `../samples/images/yellow.jpg` and `../samples/images/green.jpg` respectively.

12. Run the report to test it.

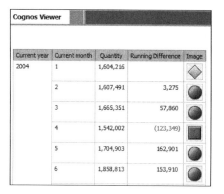

How it works...

Cognos Report Studio allows you to put the images in the report by specifying the URL of the image. The images can be anywhere on the intranet or internet. They will be displayed properly as long as the URL is accessible from Cognos application server and gateway.

In this recipe, we are using a report which already calculates the Running Difference. Hence, we just had to define conditional variable to trap different possible conditions. The **Image** component allows us to define the URL for different conditions by attaching it to the **Traffic** variable in step 8.

There's more...

In this case, though the URL of the image changes dynamically, it is not truly 100% dynamic. There are three static URLs already defined in the report and one is picked up depending on the condition.

We can also use a data item or report expression as source of the URL value. In that case, it will be totally dynamic, and based on the values coming from database; Cognos will work out the URL of the image and display it correctly.

This is useful when the image filenames and locations are stored in the database. For example, Product Catalogue kind of reports.

More info

This recipe works fine in HTML, PDF, and Excel formats.

We have used relative URLs for the images, so that report can be easily deployed to other environments where Cognos installation might be in a different location. However, we need to ensure that the images are copied in all environments in the folder mentioned in step 2.

Handling missing image issue

In the previous recipe, we saw how to add images to the report. You will be using that technique in many cases, some involving hundreds of images (For example, Product Catalogue).

There will often be a case in which database has a URL or image name, whereas the corresponding image is either missing or inaccessible. In such a case, the web browser shows an error symbol. This looks quite ugly and needs to be handled properly.

Current year	Current month	Quantity	Running Difference	Image
2004	1	1,604,216		
	2	1,607,491	3,275	
	3	1,665,351	57,860	
	4	1,542,002	(123,349)	
	5	1,704,903	162,901	
	6	1,858,813	153,910	

In this recipe, we will see how to handle this problem gracefully.

Getting ready

We will use the report prepared in previous recipe. We need to delete the `Green.jpg` file (or rename it to something else) from the server, in order to create the missing image scenario.

How to do it...

1. In the previous recipe, we added an **image object** and defined its **conditional URLs**. We need to replace that image with an **HTML Item**. For that, unlock the report objects 🔒 and delete the image component. Add an **HTML Item** in the same column.

Current year	Current month	Quantity	Running Difference	Image
<⌷ Current year>	<▲ Current month>	<Quantity>	<Running Difference>	< HTML Item >
<Current year>	<Current month>	<Quantity>	<Running Difference>	< HTML Item >

2. Select this HTML item and from the Properties pane, set its **HTML Source Variable** to 'Traffic'. (Please note that we already have this conditional variable in the last recipe).

3. Now define the HTML for different conditions. Start with 'red'. Choose 'red' from conditional explorer and define the HTML as: `<img src="../samples/images/red.jpg" alt="downsell" onError="img2txt(this)"/>`

4. For 'yellow', define the HTML as: `<img src="../samples/images/yellow.jpg" alt="No Change" onError="img2txt(this)"/>`

5. For 'green', define HTML as: `<img src="../samples/images/green.jpg" alt="Upsell" onError="img2txt(this)"/>`

6. Now go back to the **No Variable** state by double clicking on the green bar, and add another HTML item on the report. Put it just before the list.

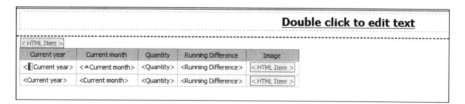

7. Define this HTML as:

```
<script>
function img2txt(img) {
txt = img.alt;
img.parentNode.innerHTML=txt;}
</script>
```

8. Now run the report to test it.

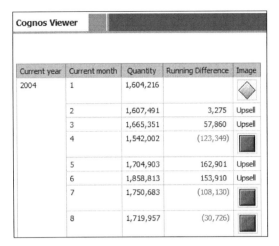

As you can see, if the image is missing, the report will now handle it gracefully and show some text instead of an error image.

How it works...

Here we are using our custom code to display the image, instead of using CRS's in-built **Image** component.

We have pulled an HTML item onto the report and defined it to display different images depending on the condition using the `<img>` tag. This tag allows us to define an alternative text and `onError` event as well. We are using the `onError` event to call our custom made JavaScript function called `img2txt`.

This function replaces the HTML item with a text which was originally defined as 'alternative text'. Hence, if `green.jpg` is missing, this function will replace it with a text item **Upsell**.

There's more...

As we are using HTML code and JavaScript in this technique, it works in HTML format only. This technique will be useful for a lot of graphical reports (dashboards, scorecards, online product catalogues, and so on).

Dynamic links to external website (Google Map example)

In this recipe, we will introduce you to the 'Hyperlink' component.

A report shows retailers information by products. It shows various fields like **Retailer name**, **Contact information**, **City**, and **Postal zone**. Business wants to have a link to Google maps that will show retailer's place on the map using the **Postal zone** information.

As the addresses might change in the backend, the technique needs to be dynamic to pick up the latest postal zone.

Getting ready

Create a simple list report that shows Retailers information by Product lines.

How to do it...

1. From the 'Insertable Objects' toolbox, drag a hyperlink object onto the report as a new column.

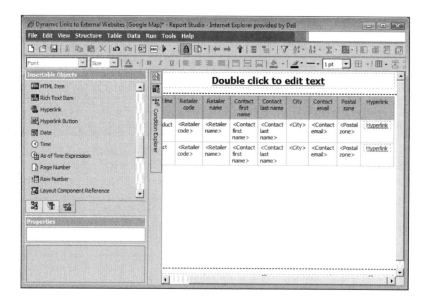

2. Change its **Text** property to **Map**. Set the **URL Source Type** to **Report Expression** and define the report expression as follows:

```
'http://maps.google.com/maps?q=' + [Query1].[City]
```

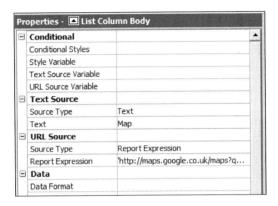

3. Run the report to test it.

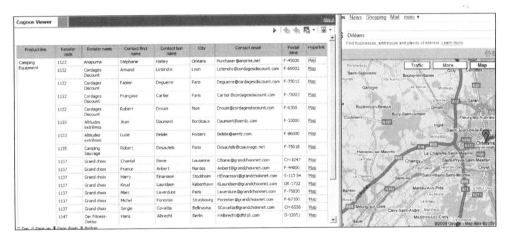

As you can see, there is a link for each retailer record. If you *Shift+click* on the link, it will open the Google map for corresponding postal zone in a new window.

How it works...

Here we are using the 'Hyperlink' component of CRS. We can define the URL as any static link.

However, for our requirements, we have defined a report expression. This allows us to provide a dynamic link which picks up the latest postal zone from the database. We are passing the postal zone to Google Maps as part of a URL.

The hyperlink component works in HTML as well as Excel and PDF formats of report. This object currently does not have the property to define whether the link target should open in a new window or the same window. Just clicking on the link, opens the target in same window; whereas *Shift+click* opens in a new window.

There's more...

You can use this technique to call any external website that accepts parameters within a URL. You can pass multiple parameters too.

Alternating drill link

In this recipe, we will learn about a limitation of drill link and overcoming it using **Render Variable**.

There is a crosstab report which shows sales quantity by month and order method. We need to provide drill-through facility from the intersection. However, the drill-through target needs to be different, depending on the order method.

If order method is e-mail, the drill-through from intersection should go to a report called 'Alternating Drill Link—Drill Report 2'. For all other order methods, it should go to 'Alternating Drill Link—Drill Report 1'.

Getting ready

Create a crosstab report to serve as the main report. Drag **Month** (shipment) on rows, **Order method** on columns and **Sales Quantity** on the intersection.

Create two list reports to serve as drill reports. In the sample provided with this book, we have used two list reports for this. One accepts the **Order method** and **Month**. The other accepts only month and is designed to work for the order method 'E-mail'.

How to do it...

1. As already learnt in Chapter 2, create a drill through to first drill the report from the crosstab intersection.

Quantity	<#Order method#>	<#Order method#>
<#Month#>	✛ <#1234#>	✛ <#1234#>
<#Month#>	✛ <#1234#>	✛ <#1234#>

2. Now make sure that the report objects are unlocked. Select the intersection text item (which now looks like hyperlink as there is already a drill-through defined). Hold the *Ctrl* key down and drag the text to its right within a cell.

3. This should create a copy of the text item within that cell and will look like the following:

Quantity	<#Order method#>	<#Order method#>
<#Month#>	✛<#1234#> ✛<#1234#>	✛<#1234#> ✛<#1234#>
<#Month#>	✛<#1234#> ✛<#1234#>	✛<#1234#> ✛<#1234#>

4. Now select this copy of the text item. Hit the drill-through button to open definitions. Delete the existing drill-through to first report. Create a new drill to a second report.

    So, now we have two text items in the cell, each going to different drill reports.

5. Create a string type of Conditional Variable. Define it as:

```
if ([Query1].[Order method] = 'E-mail') then ('E-mail')
else ('Other')
```

Call it **OrderMethod** and define the two values to be **E-mail** and **Other**.

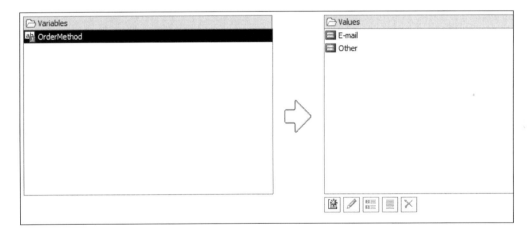

6. Now go back to the report page. Select the first text item from intersection. Open its **Render Variable** property. Choose the **OrderMethod** variable and select to **Render for: Other**.

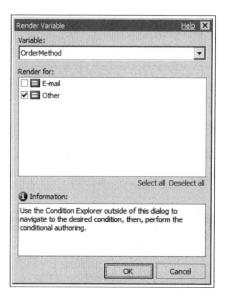

7. Similarly, define **Render Variable** for the second text item, but choose to **Render for: E-mail**.

8. Run the report to test it. You will see that clicking on the intersection numbers opens first drill report for any order method other than E-mail. Whereas for the numbers under E-mail, the second drill report opens.

How it works...

First, let me explain to you the limitation here. CRS allows us to define multiple drill targets for an item. However, there is no facility to define a conditional target. So, if we define two targets, Cognos will ask users to select one at the run-time.

In our scenario, we want Cognos to go straight to one of the two targets depending on the order method condition. For that we are using the Render variable property.

Render variable

This property allows us to attach a conditional variable to the report object and define the conditions for which the object will be rendered.

This works best with String variables. For a Boolean type of conditional variable, rendering is possible only for 'Yes'.

Instead of defining two targets on same text item, we are creating two text items and controlling their rendering.

There's more...

Even with String type of conditional variable, rendering cannot be defined for the default (Other) condition. Hence, we had to define our own 'Other' condition.

Showing tool tip on reports

A report shows all time sales quantity by product names. As this report is used online (HTML format in Internet Explorer), business thinks it will be handy to show **Product description** as tooltip on the product names. When the user hovers their mouse pointer over **Product name**, a tooltip should appear, describing the product.

Getting ready

Create a simple list report with Product name, Product description, and Sales Quantity as columns.

How to do it...

1. We don't want to show the **Product description** as column, but want to use the data item in further steps. So, select **Product description** column and cut it using *Ctrl+X*. Confirm that the Product description data item is still present in Query1 by checking in **Query Explorer**.

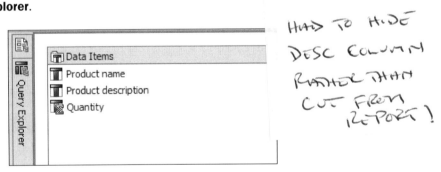

HAD TO HIDE DESC COLUMN RATHER THAN CUT FROM REPORT !

2. On the report page, unlock the report objects by hitting unlock button.

3. Insert an **HTML Item** in **Product name** column, just before the text item. Insert another **HTML Item** after the text item. This will look like the following screenshot:

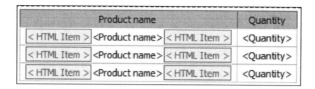

4. Define the first HTML item as a **Report Expression** and define it as:

```
'<span title="' + [Query1].[Product description] + '">'
```

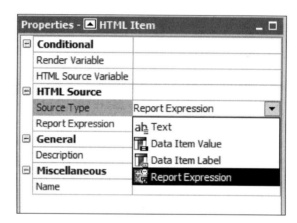

5. Define the second HTML item as a **Text**: `</span>`

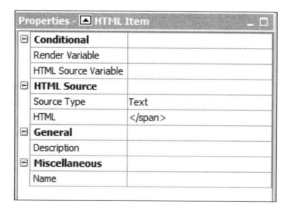

6. Run the report to test it.

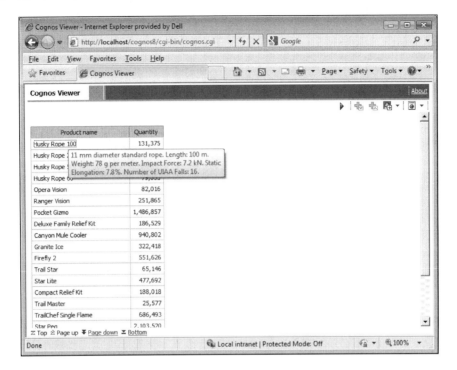

How it works...

Here we are using our familiar and very useful HTML tag called `<span>`. We used it earlier for applying JavaScript for prompt manipulation. In this recipe, we are wrapping the product name within a span and defining its **Title** to be **Product description**.

When report is run in web browser, the title is shown as **Tooltip**.

There's more...

Once you define the span, you can do much more to the item. For example, overriding the mouse events. Please refer to HTML guides for this.

See also

Read about using SPAN to manipulate the prompt control in previous chapter (*Chapter 3, Tips and Tricks: JavaScript—Prompt page*).

Achieving minimum column width

A report shows sales quantity by product line and order method. The order methods are displayed as columns. When the crosstab is wider than the IE window, Cognos automatically shrinks the column width instead of showing the horizontal scrollbar.

Hence, you will notice that some columns are wider and some are narrower, depending on the data. For example, the **Fax** and **Mail** columns in the following screenshot are narrower than the **Telephone** column.

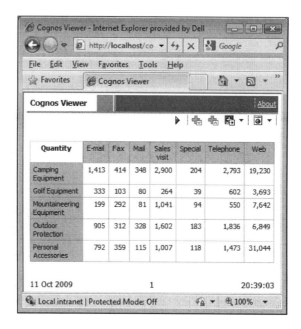

In this recipe, we will see a technique to achieve minimum column width for columns. When the crosstab is wider than the page width, the columns will not shrink more than a certain limit and a horizontal scroll bar will be provided automatically.

Getting ready

Create a crosstab report with product line on rows, order method on columns, and sales quantity as intersection.

Copy the `invisible.gif` supplied with this book to the Cognos server under `{Cognos Installation}\webcontent\samples\images` folder.

How to do it...

1. Unlock the report objects using **Unlock** button. 🔒

2. Drag a new block object from the insertable objects toolbox, to the columns titles just under the order method text item.

3. Now drag an image object inside this block. The report will now look like this:

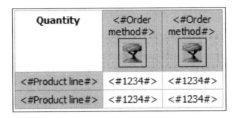

4. Set the Image URL to: `../samples/images/invisible.gif`.

5. Run the report to test it.

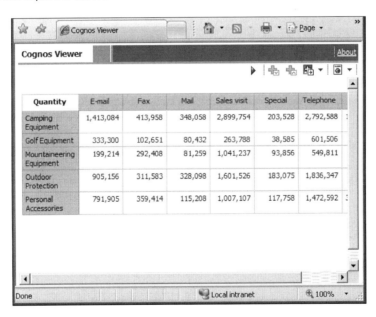

Notice that the **Fax** and **Mail** columns are no longer shrunk and a horizontal scrollbar has appeared as a crosstab and is wider than screen.

How it works...

CRS allows you to define the size of report columns. However, that size works mainly as a guideline. If the contents are larger, the columns are automatically stretched, which is good. However, Cognos also shrinks the columns that don't have much data, if the report width is larger than the web browser width.

In short, there are no specific settings for the minimum column width. In this recipe, we achieve it by placing an invisible GIF image in the column titles.

Merged cells in Excel output

There is a list report with many columns. The report shows the title in page header. Users mostly access this report in Excel format.

When the output is generated, Cognos puts the output in the first cell (A1). This stretches the A column.

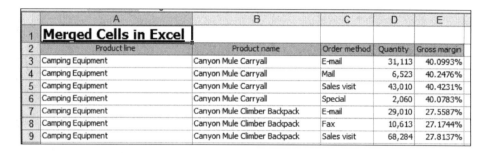

In this recipe, we will see how to get Cognos to generate merged cells so that the columns are not stretched.

Getting ready

Create a simple list report. Put a report title in the page header.

How to do it...

1. Insert a **Table** from the 'Insertable objects' pane into the report header.

2. Set the **Number of columns** to **4**. Keep **Number of rows** at **1**. Hit **OK**.

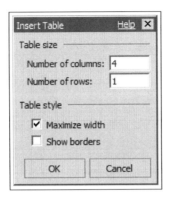

3. Now select the first cell of the table. Hold down *Shift* key and select the last cell of the table. This should select all the cells.

4. From the menu, select **Table | Merge Cells**. This will merge four cells into one.

5. Now unlock the report objects. Select the report title and drag it inside the table.

6. Change the text font and size appropriately.

7. Run the report in Excel to test it. As you can see in the following screenshot, the title will now be shown in merged cells and hence the first column won't be stretched.

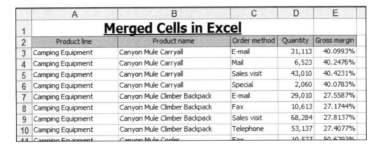

How it works...

When we merge the cells of a table, this is remembered in the report specification in the form of column span. In our example, the report spec says `<tableCell colSpan="4">`. When the report runs in Excel form, this is properly translated into merged cells.

Not many developers know about this feature, but it is a very useful one. After reading this, you will use it in many real-life scenarios.

Worksheet name in Excel output

A report has three list report objects (Sales by products, Sales by region, Sales by order method). Users prefer to access it in Excel format.

They want the three reports to be populated on three different sheets and each sheet should be named appropriately.

Getting ready

Create a report with three list report objects and pull appropriate columns in each.

How to do it...

1. Open **Page Explorer** and add two new **Page** objects.

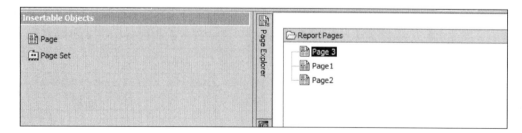

2. Select each of them and change their name from properties to as shown in the following screenshot:

3. Now cut the list objects from the first page and paste in the appropriate report page.
4. Run the report in Excel to test it.

As you can see, Cognos produces three sheets with the names same as what we defined for 'Page name' (with an auto-incrementing number appended). Each sheet will show the list object we placed in corresponding page.

How it works...

When we generate the report in Excel format, the name of worksheet matches the name of page in CRS. A number is appended to make sure that names are unique. This is useful for long reports where one page will span multiple sheets.

There's more...

There is a lot of demand for dynamic sheet names. For example, if we create a page set for products so that Cognos will create one sheet per product; then we expect to name the sheets by products.

However, there is currently no facility to define such dynamic names (data item or expression). Some users have requested this enhancement to IBM and this feature might be added in the future version of CRS.

Conditional column titles

This recipe is meant to introduce you to the **Text source variable** property.

There is a crosstab report that shows sales quantity by order method (rows) and months (columns). We need to conditionally show full month names or short names depending on user's selection on the prompt page.

Getting ready

Create a crosstab report with **Order Method | Order Method** on rows, **Time (ship Date) | Month (Ship Date)** on columns and **Sales fact | Quantity** in the intersection.

Create a value prompt on the prompt page with following specification:

- ▸ Static choices: Full name, Short name
- ▸ Parameter name: choice
- ▸ User Interface (UI): Radio button group

How to do it...

1. Go to **Conditional Explorer** and create a Boolean variable. Call it as **Is_FullName** and define it as: `ParamDisplayValue('choice') = 'Full Name'`.

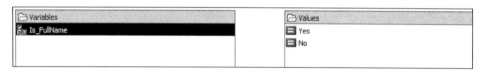

2. Now go to the report page and select **<Month>** from column titles. Set its **Text Source** variable to **Is_FullName**.

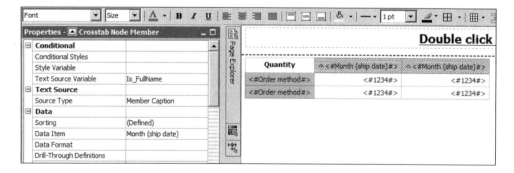

3. From **Conditional Explorer**, choose **Yes** condition for the variable. This will allow you to define the text for columns. Set the **Source Type** to **Data Item Value**. Choose **Month (ship date)** as **Data Item Value**.

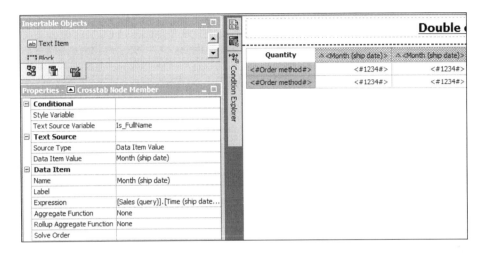

4. Now choose **No** condition for the Boolean variable. Set the **Source Type** for **<Month (ship date)>** column to report expression. Define the expression as:

    ```
    substring([Query1].[Month (ship date)],1,3).
    ```

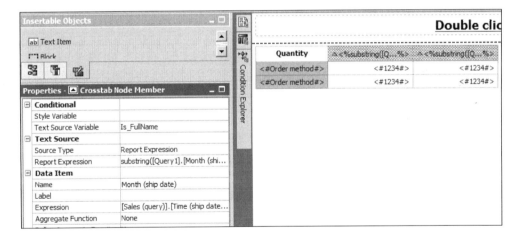

5. Run the report to test it.

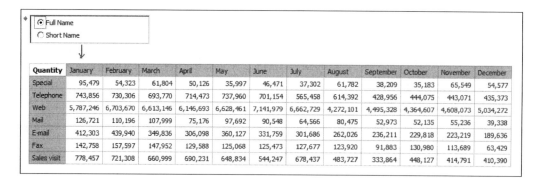

Quantity	January	February	March	April	May	June	July	August	September	October	November	December
Special	95,479	54,323	61,804	50,126	35,997	46,471	37,302	61,782	38,209	35,183	65,549	54,577
Telephone	743,856	730,306	693,770	714,473	737,960	701,154	565,458	614,392	428,956	444,075	443,071	435,373
Web	5,787,246	6,703,670	6,613,146	6,146,693	6,628,461	7,141,979	6,662,729	4,272,101	4,495,328	4,364,607	4,608,073	5,034,272
Mail	126,721	110,196	107,999	75,176	97,692	90,548	64,566	80,475	52,973	52,135	55,236	39,338
E-mail	412,303	439,940	349,836	306,098	360,127	331,759	301,686	262,026	236,211	229,818	223,219	189,636
Fax	142,758	157,597	147,952	129,588	125,068	125,473	127,677	123,920	91,883	130,980	113,689	63,429
Sales visit	778,457	721,308	660,999	690,231	648,834	544,247	678,437	483,727	333,864	448,127	414,791	410,390

How it works...

Here we are using the Text source variable property to link the text being shown in columns titles to the conditional variable.

Once the variable is defined, for each condition, we can define a static text, a data item value, or a report expression to be shown in the column title. This way we can conditionally change the column titles. The same can be applied to row titles as well.

5
XML Editing

In this chapter, we will cover the following:

- ▸ Quickly changing drill links
- ▸ Copy-pasting drill links
- ▸ Removing references to old packages or items
- ▸ XML hidden gems—row formatting tag

Introduction

This chapter will show some advanced techniques that involve changing the XML specification of a report outside of Report Studio. This is a common practice amongst experienced report writers. It often saves a lot of time and also provides some functionality that is not available in Report Studio.

You should preferably have an XML editor application for this. I have used Visual Studio for this. The advantages of using an XML editor are visual aids to help XML editing, automatic tag completion, tree like expand-collapse functionality, and easy search and replace. However, if you don't have one, you can also use any generic text editor for these recipes, for example, Textpad or Notepad.

If you don't know anything about XML at all, it would be worth reading about it on the Internet. There are websites like www.xmlfiles.com and www.w3schools.com/xml that are good for basic understanding and practice. After reading about XML and following the recipes step-by-step, you will not only be able to perform the actions covered in this chapter, but you will have confidence to do more XML editing of reports on your own.

It is advisable to take a backup of the original report before replacing it with an XML modified one outside Report Studio.

Quickly changing drill targets

While the project is in the development stage, many things change. Files are moved, folders are renamed, and sometimes requirements change. This often results in re-work.

Assume that a crosstab report has been designed to drill to a target report from intersection. The drill target report accepts many parameters and their mapping is already done. However, because of some changes in business requirement, the drill from intersection now needs to go to another report. That report is already designed to accept the same parameters; we only need to change the target in the main report.

In this recipe, we will see how to quickly change the target report for a drill-through definition, without the need to map the parameters again.

Getting ready

Create a crosstab report shown as follows and save it as '5.1 Drill from crosstab intersection'.

Quantity	<#Order method#>	<#Order method#>
<#Month (ship date)#>	✥ <#1234#>	✥ <#1234#>
<#Month (ship date)#>	✥ <#1234#>	✥ <#1234#>

Create drill-through link from the crosstab intersection to a list report and pass multiple values. This list report can be just a simple one shown as follows. Save this report as '5.1 Drill from crosstab intersection Drill 2'.

Month (ship date)	Order method	Product name	Quantity	Unit cost
<Month (ship date)>	<Order method>	<Product name>	<Quantity>	<Unit cost>
<Month (ship date)>	<Order method>	<Product name>	<Quantity>	<Unit cost>
<Month (ship date)>	<Order method>	<Product name>	<Quantity>	<Unit cost>

Create one more copy of the above report and save it as '5.1 Drill from crosstab intersection Drill 1'.

So, now we have the following folder structure:

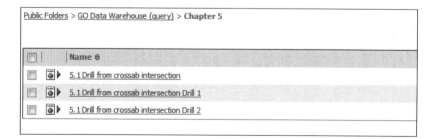

The main report (5.1 Drill from crosstab intersection) has been designed to call '5.1 Drill from crosstab intersection Drill 2'. We will change it to call 'Drill 1' instead by editing XML. This way we will not have to define the parameter mapping again and it will save the developer's time.

How to do it...

1. Open the main report in Report Studio.

2. Unlock the report objects and select crosstab intersection. Hit the'drill-through' button on the toolbar and examine the drill-target.

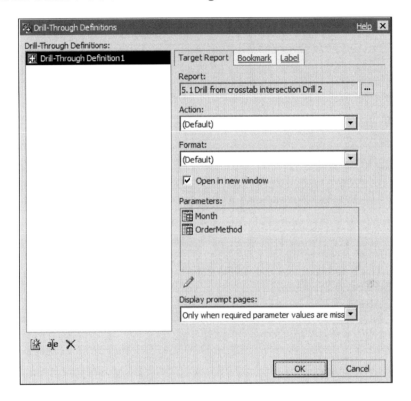

Notice that the drill through has been designed to go to **5.1 Drill from crosstab intersection Drill 2** and passes two parameters called **Month** and **OrderMethod**. In real life, you will usually have many parameters passed.

3. Now close the dialog. Choose **Tools | Copy Report to Clipboard** option from menu. This will copy the XML specification of the report on clipboard.

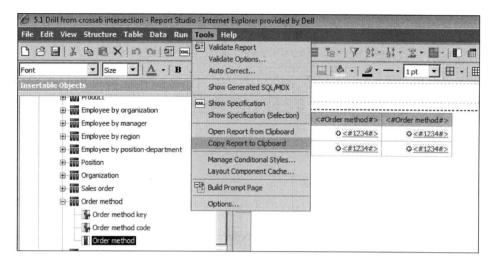

4. Open any text editor or XML editor, and paste the XML spec.

5. Now go to Cognos Connection. For the **5.1 Drill from Crosstab intersection Drill 1** report, click on **Set Properties** button.

6. Click on the **View search path** link.

7. A dialog-box will pop up with following information. Select the **Search path** and copy it.

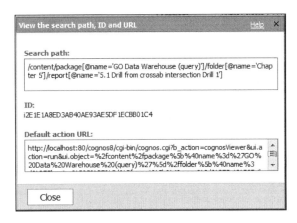

8. Go back to the XML specification pasted in the text or XML editor. Replace all the report paths referring to `Drill 2` with that of `Drill 1`. In our recipe, we will search for all instances of :

```
'/content/package[@name='GO Data Warehouse (query)']/folder[@
name='Chapter 5']/report[@name='5.1 Drill from crossab
intersection Drill 2']'
```

and replace them with :

```
'/content/package[@name='GO Data Warehouse (query)']/folder[@
name='Chapter 5']/report[@name='5.1 Drill from crossab
intersection Drill 1']'
```

9. Now copy the whole XML specification (modified one) on the clipboard.

10. Go back to Report Studio and choose the **Tools | Open Report from Clipboard** option.

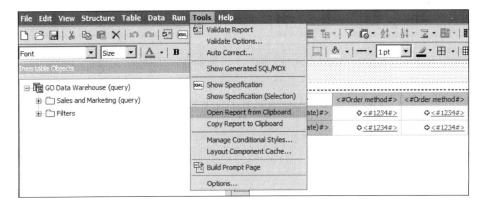

11. Check the drill through target again. It should be changed to **Drill 1** with all the parameter still mapped correctly.

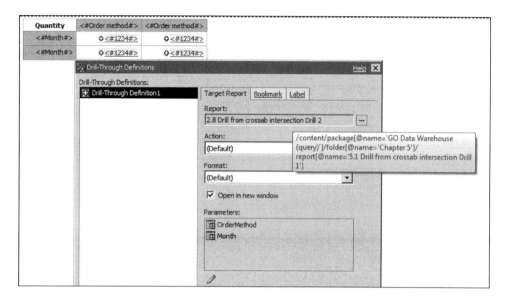

12. Save the report as the main report.

How it works...

In Report Studio, if you change the target report for an existing drill-through definition, then it wants to redefine the parameter mapping. Here we are achieving that without the need to redefine the mapping.

For that we are directly modifying the XML specification of the report. When we copy a report to clipboard, its XML spec is copied. We then edit it in an editor, and replace all the references to 'Drill 2' report with 'Drill 1' report.

Finally, we copy the modified the XML back into Report Studio and find that the drill target is successfully changed.

There's more...

It is advisable to use an XML Editor rather than normal Text Editor as it allows you to understand the tags better and hence reduce the chances of errors.

You can explore `<reportDrills>` tag more and try changing different properties/members within that.

Copy-pasting drill link

A crosstab report shows Sales Quantity by quarter (rows), Product line (columns) and Order method (columns). The report has several filters.

There is a drill-through report which is to be called from the report columns, that is, product line and order method. When called, all the filter values are to be passed.

In this recipe, we will see how to define the drill-through and parameter mapping once and then copy-paste it for other drills—hence saving the development time.

Getting ready

Create a crosstab report to be used as main report in the following format:

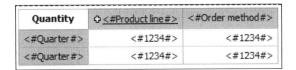

Define all the prompts and filters on main report.

Now create a drill report that will accept all these parameters and additional information like **Product line** and **Order method**. This is shown as follows:

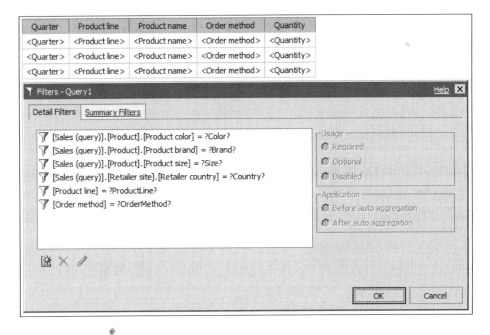

How to do it...

1. We will start by defining the drill-through from Product line columns. Do it manually from Report Studio in a conventional way. Map all the parameters appropriately.

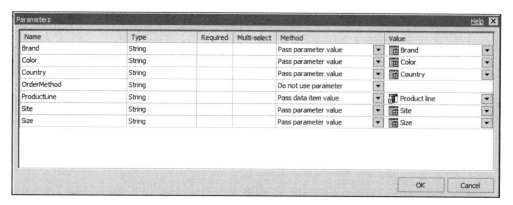

2. Now select the Order method column title. Create a drill-through link and select the target report. Don't do the parameter mapping. We are not doing the mapping here as we will copy-paste it in later steps and hence save development time.

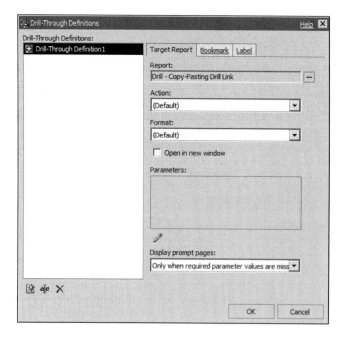

3. Select **Copy report to clipboard** from menu and paste it in a new file in the XML editor. I used Visual Studio for this.

4. Look for `<drillTargetContext>` tag. This will help you find the correct drill from Product line (which has all the mapping done).

```
<reportDrills>
    <reportDrill name="Drill-Through Definition1">
        <drillLabel>
            <dataSource>
                <staticValue/>
            </dataSource>
        </drillLabel>
        <drillTarget showInNewWindow="true">
            <reportPath path="/content/package[@name='GO Data Warehouse
                <XMLAttributes>
                    <XMLAttribute name="ReportName" value="Drill - Copy
                    <XMLAttribute name="class" value="report" output="n
                </XMLAttributes>
            </reportPath>
            <drillLinks>
                <drillLink>
                    <drillTargetContext>
                        <parameterContext parameter="Brand"/>
                    </drillTargetContext>
```

5. Copy the whole `<reportDrill>` element from above (that is, everything from `<reportDrill>` tag to `</reportDrill>` tag).

```
<dataSource>
    <memberCaption/>
</dataSource>
<reportDrills>
    <reportDrill name="Drill-Through D">...</reportDrill>
</reportDrills>
<style>
    <defaultStyles>
        <defaultStyle refStyle="hy"/>
```

6. Now look for the `<reportDrills>` tag and search for the one that relates to order method. This one doesn't have the mapping defined.

```
<crosstabNode>
    <crosstabNodeMembers>
        <crosstabNodeMember refDataItem="Order method" edgeLocation="e2">
            <style>...</style>
            <contents>
                <textItem>
                    <dataSource>...</dataSource>
                    <reportDrills>
                        <reportDrill name="Drill-Through Definition1">
                            <drillLabel>
                                <dataSource>
                                    <staticValue/>
                                </dataSource>
                            </drillLabel>
                            <drillTarget>
                                <reportPath path="/content/package[@name='GO Da
                                    <XMLAttributes>
                                        <XMLAttribute name="ReportName" value="
                                        <XMLAttribute name="class" value="repor
                                    </XMLAttributes>
                                </reportPath>
                            </drillTarget>
                        </reportDrill>
                    </reportDrills>
```

7. Replace the existing `<reportDrill>` element with the one copied in step 5.

8. Copy whole XML specification back on clipboard and open in Report Studio. Examine the drill-through from **Order method** column titles.

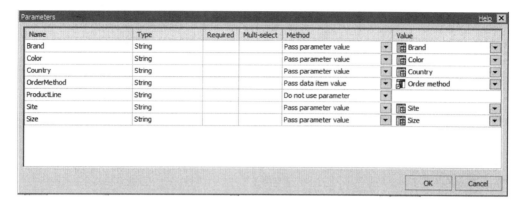

You will see that the mapping is now successfully copied. Make appropriate changes to it, if required. Here, we will pass Order method instead of Product line.

9. Run the report to test it.

How it works...

This recipe is extremely useful when the report has many drill links and lots of parameters to be passed in each drill.

We define the parameter mapping for one drill link which gets saved in corresponding `<reportDrill>` element. Then we define other drill links without doing the parameter mapping. Finally, we copy the XML elements in the editor which in turn copies the parameter mapping across.

There's more...

This recipe might look tedious at first glance, but once you practice it, you will realize that it is useful in big reports with loads of drill links. Also, once you examine the `<reportDrills>` element carefully from the XML, you will know how Cognos Report Studio stores the drilling information. This will be useful in writing your own utilities to parse or modify the report specification.

Removing references to old package and namespaces

As part of development, Framework Model might need changes. Often the package names, namespaces names, and query subject names are changed. Sometimes when report is moved to another environment, such differences are encountered. This results in error; and needs every data item to be redefined.

In this recipe, we will see how to quickly change all the references without redefining all data items.

Getting ready

Take any report that is working fine and verifying without errors. We will take one report based on the 'GO Data Warehouse (query)' package.

How to do it...

1. Open the framework model for 'GO Data Warehouse (query)' package. Change the name of the namespace being used by the report. Here we will change the **Sales(query)** namespace to **Sales Renamed**.

2. Rename the package 'GO Data Warehouse (query)' to 'GO Data Warehouse Renamed' and publish it.

3. Now open the report and change its package connection to 'GO Data Warehouse Renamed'. This will start the report validation and will return with errors.

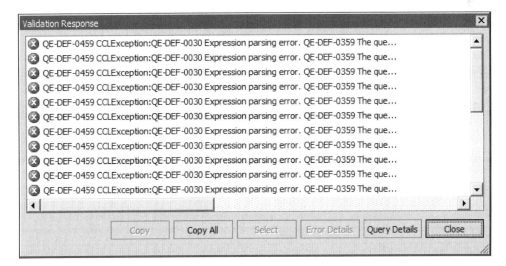

4. Examine the error detail and you will notice that it has reference to the namespace that is now renamed.

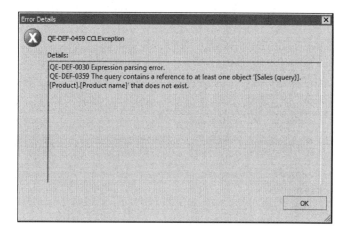

5. Now copy the report to the clipboard and paste it in your XML editor.

6. Replace all instances of [Sales (Query)] with [Sales Renamed].

Copy the report back to clipboard and open in Report Studio.

7. Verify the report. It should validate with no errors.

How it works...

The data items are stored in the report specification in the following format:

```
[Namespace Name].[Query Subject].[Query Item]
```

The folder names are not stored. Hence, if folder names are changed in the Framework Model, the reports can function fine without any change. However, if the Namespace, Query Subject, or Query Item is renamed, report needs to be updated.

Here, namespace is renamed. This is referenced many times in the report (in every data item). Hence, manually changing it in report studio is a tedious job. Hence, we are opening the report specification in XML editor and doing a simple search and replace operation to change all the references.

A hidden gem in XML—row level formatting

As you know now, a Cognos Report is an XML definition. When you create or update a report in Report Studio, the corresponding XML tags are added to or modified in the report specification. However, it is possible to directly add or modify XML tags that are not visible from the studio as an object or property.

In this recipe, we will see how to define crosstab row level formatting in the XML to save the development and maintenance time.

There is a crosstab report with many measures on columns. The business wants to highlight the rows which belong to costly products (>25 units). Instead of defining conditional formatting for every column, we will modify the XML here to directly define row level formatting.

Getting ready

Create a report with product name on rows and various measures on columns, shown as follows:

	<#Quantity#>	<#Unit price#>	<#Unit sale price#>	<#Gross margin#>	<#Revenue#>	<#Gross profit#>	<#Product cost#>	<#Planned revenue#>
<#Product name#>	<#1234#>	<#1234#>	<#1234#>	<#1234#>	<#1234#>	<#1234#>	<#1234#>	<#1234#>
<#Product name#>	<#1234#>	<#1234#>	<#1234#>	<#1234#>	<#1234#>	<#1234#>	<#1234#>	<#1234#>

How to do it...

1. Define a conditional variable of Boolean type to identify costly products (which are to be highlighted in the report).

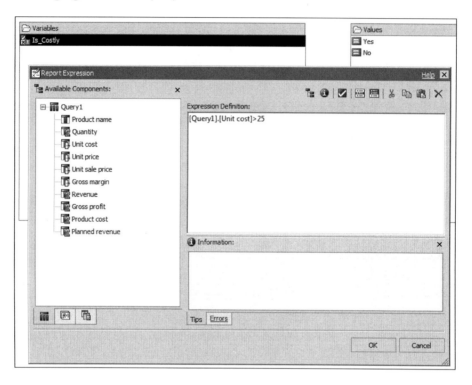

   Call this variable as `Is_Costly`.

2. Now select the first column **Quantity**. Attach the conditional variable `Is_Costly` to it as **Style variable**. Define the appropriate formatting for this column for both the conditions (Yes and No). We have already talked about defining conditional styles in prior chapters.

3. Now copy the report to clipboard and paste in a new file in an XML editor. I have used Visual Studio for this purpose.

4. Run a search for `<conditionalStyles>` tag. You will find this element under **Quantity** data item.

5. Copy the whole element, that is from `<conditionalStyles>` to `</conditionalStyles>`.

```
<crosstabIntersections>
    <crosstabIntersection row="e1" column="e2">
        <conditionalStyles>
            <conditionalStyleCases refVariable="Is_Costly">
                <conditionalStyle refVariableValue="1">
                    <CSS value="background-color:lime"/>
                </conditionalStyle>
            </conditionalStyleCases>
            <conditionalStyleDefault>
                <CSS value="background-color:yellow"/>
            </conditionalStyleDefault>
        </conditionalStyles>
    </crosstabIntersection>
</crosstabIntersections>
</crosstab>
```

6. Now locate the `<crosstabRows>` element. You will see that it has a
   `<crosstabNodeMember>` defined for product name.

```
<crosstabRows>
    <crosstabNode>
        <crosstabNodeMembers>
            <crosstabNodeMember refDataItem="Product name" edgeLocation="e1">
                <style>...</style>
                <contents>...</contents>

                <factCell/>

                <propertyList>
                    <propertyItem refDataItem="Unit cost"/>
                </propertyList>
            </crosstabNodeMember>

        </crosstabNodeMembers>
```

7. Replace the empty `<factCell/>` with the following code:

   ```
   <factCell>
   </factCell>
   ```

8. Now paste the `<conditionalStyles>` tag copied in step 5 within the `<factCell>`
   element. The code will now look like this.

```
<crosstabRows>
    <crosstabNode>
        <crosstabNodeMembers>
            <crosstabNodeMember refDataItem="Product name" edgeLocation="e1">
                <style>...</style>
                <contents>...</contents>

                <factCell>
                    <conditionalStyles>
                        <conditionalStyleCases refVariable="Is_Costly">
                            <conditionalStyle refVariableValue="1">
                                <CSS value="background-color:lime"/>
                            </conditionalStyle>
                        </conditionalStyleCases>
                        <conditionalStyleDefault>
                            <CSS value="background-color:yellow"/>
                        </conditionalStyleDefault>
                    </conditionalStyles>
                </factCell>

                <propertyList>
                    <propertyItem refDataItem="Unit cost"/>
                </propertyList>
            </crosstabNodeMember>

        </crosstabNodeMembers>
```

9. Copy the whole XML back on clipboard and open in Report Studio.

10. Run the report to test it.

	Quantity	Unit price	Unit sale price	Gross margin	Revenue	Gross profit	Product cost	Planned revenue
Aloe Relief	159,547	5.23	4.89	59.1524%	769,757.23	463,426.99	306,330.24	834,430.81
Astro Pilot	171,914	173.08	173.08	37.4965%	26,810,024	10,056,132.11	16,753,891.89	26,810,024
Auto Pilot	25,369	235.00	235.00	34.9038%	5,961,715	2,081,421.45	3,880,293.55	5,961,715
Bear Edge	327,519	40.52	39.35	40.2015%	12,893,464.19	5,186,942.12	7,706,522.07	13,271,069.88
Bear Survival Edge	119,662	92.29	86.68	47.1538%	10,329,654.58	4,839,887.58	5,489,767.00	11,043,605.98
Bella	396,690	68.22	68.14	45.4707%	26,876,327.5	12,151,382.7	14,724,944.80	27,039,897.5
Blue Steel Max Putter	235,198	180.63	151.51	41.8584%	37,494,513.8	16,416,357.93	21,078,155.87	42,483,814.74
Blue Steel Putter	240,014	90.95	79.30	47.7739%	19,637,204.32	9,748,627.52	9,888,576.80	21,961,392.5

As you can see, the whole row is formatted based on the condition.

How it works...

In Report Studio, there is no option to select and modify whole row in crosstab. Hence, if we want to do any row level formatting, we need to do it for each column.

However, if you examine the report XML, you will notice that it has an element for fact cells under crosstab rows. Here we are overriding this element and defining our own style to be applied for every fact cell within that row.

Instead of manually writing the whole conditional style code, we have first applied Conditional style on one column (quantity) and then copied the same under "Crosstab rows" so that it is applied on all the columns.

There's more...

This recipe will save your development time as you don't have to define the conditional styling for every column. Also, in future if styling needs to be changed, it can be changed from just one place than doing so for every column. Hence, it will save maintenance time as well.

You can also experiment with the `<crosstabColumns>` tag to style whole column, when there are multiple members on rows.

See also

For conditional formatting basics, please refer to *Chapter 1, Report Authoring Basic Concepts*.

6
Writing Printable Reports

In this chapter, we will cover the following:

- ▶ Container size and rows per page
- ▶ Eliminating orphan rows
- ▶ Defining page orientation and size (and overriding them for one page)
- ▶ Avoiding page title repetition
- ▶ Horizontal pagination
- ▶ Choosing output format from prompt
- ▶ Choosing the right colors
- ▶ Defining page sets
- ▶ A warning about HTML items and JavaScripts

Introduction

The business' reports need to be printed or generated and saved in PDF for sharing and printing. This part is often ignored during defining the technical specification and actual development of reports. This chapter will give you some tips and show you the options within the Studio that you should use during development, to make the reports better printable.

Container size and rows per page

In this recipe, we will examine options around data container size and rows per page.

Getting ready

Create a simple list report with **Product** attribute's and sales **Quantity** as columns.

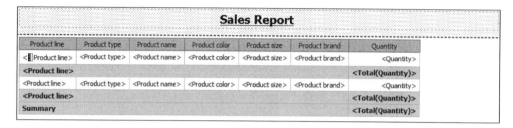

Define grouping and aggregation as shown previously.

How to do it...

1. On the report page, click on any column from the list.
2. Using ancestor button, select whole list in the **Properties** tab.
3. Set **Rows Per Page** to **50**.

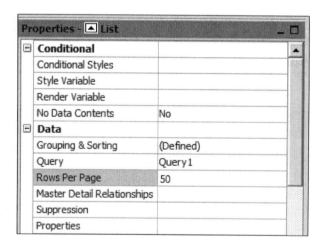

4.   Now open the **Size & Overflow** property. Set the width of list to **100%**.

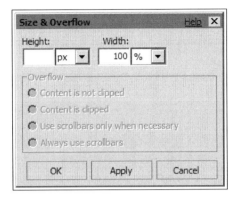

5.   Run the report in HTML and PDF formats to test it.

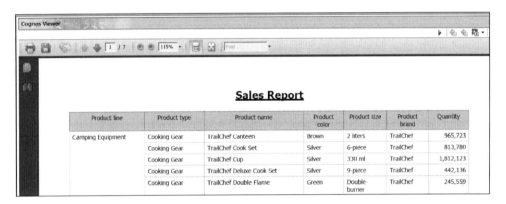

6.   Save the report for use in the next recipe.

How it works...

You will notice in the output that the HTML report shows 50 rows per page. There is a scrollbar on the right for browsing the report page. Whereas in PDF, it only shows a page-full of rows per page.

In practice, the two most frequently used output formats by the users are HTML and PDF. HTML is great for interactivity and speed, whereas PDF is useful for printing.

When reports are run in HTML format, by default, they show 20 rows per page. Users can then click on the **Next Page** link to go to the next page. This can sometimes be tedious as it is easier to see more information on one page and scroll down, than to click the **Next link** every time. Here we achieve that by setting the **Rows per Page** property of the list container. This ensures there are less user-clicks required to browse the whole data.

The beauty of this feature is that it doesn't affect the PDF output. The PDF generated will still show only appropriate number of rows to fill each page. Hence, the text is still readable and report is printable.

The **Size and Overflow** property of the list is also very useful to make it presentable. Here we are setting the width to 100% so that the list is stretched to cover the page width. The columns are appropriately distributed across the page width. This is commonly used in business reporting, though some companies prefer non-stretched, centre-aligned lists.

Please note that this feature is not particular if users would prefer the report output in Excel format because this will spread the report over multiple sheets, each having only the specified number of rows.

There's more...

Please take your time to explore other **Size and Overflow** properties. The following piece of information is found in the Cognos Help and gives something to experiment for.

Option	Description
Height	Sets the height of the object.
Width	Sets the width of the object.
Content is not clipped	If the contents of the block exceed the height or width of the block, the block automatically resizes to fit the contents.
Content is clipped	If the contents of the block exceed the height or width of the block, the content is clipped. **Note:** The clipped content still exists. It is just not visible in the block.
Use scrollbars only when necessary	If the contents of the block exceed the height or width of the block, scrollbars are added to the block.
Always use scrollbars	Scrollbars are added to the block.

Eliminating orphan rows

When a grouped report with a header or footer is generated with equal number of rows per page; it might create some orphan rows. Please see the following screenshot:

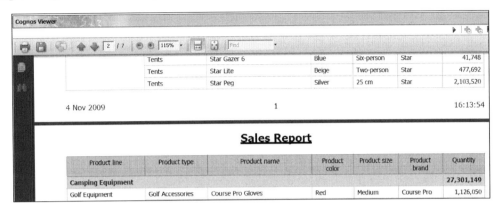

As you can see the totals for **Camping Equipment** has gone on the next page and looks like an orphan. In this recipe, we will see how to solve such issues of orphan rows.

Getting ready

We will use the report that we created in the previous recipe.

How to do it...

1. Open the report from the location where you saved it in the previous recipe. In Cognos Report Studio, open the report page. Select any column in the list.

2. Using ancestor selector, select the **List** object.

3. Open the **Pagination** property and set **Keep with footer** to **5**.

4. Run the report to test it.

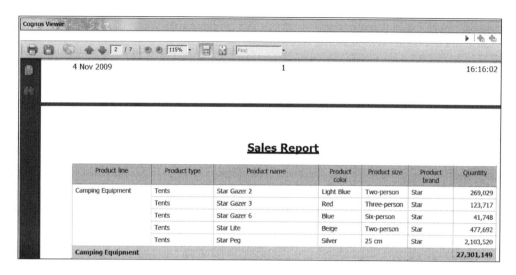

How it works...

As you can see in the last screenshot, Cognos now moved 5 rows on the next page to connect to the **Camping Equipment** totals.

The property **Keep with footer** specifies how many rows need to be with footer so that it doesn't hang out as an orphan. This setting will take precedence over the **Rows per Page**.

There's more...

If there is a group header, you can also use the **Keep with header** property to make sure that header row is not left an orphan.

Defining page orientation and size (also override for one page)

In this recipe, we will see how to specify page orientation and size to achieve better print-outs. We will also see how to override these settings for certain pages.

Getting ready

Use the report created in the previous recipe.

Add a new report page called **Title** and use it to define the title page at the beginning of the report.

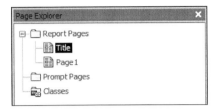

How to do it...

1. Open the report in Report Studio. From the menu, choose **File | PDF Page Setup**.

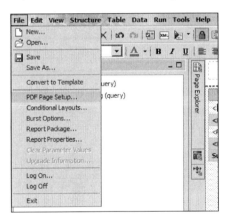

2. Define the orientation as **Landscape** and **Paper Size** to **Letter**.

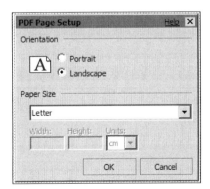

3. Now open **Page Explorer** and open the **Title** page.

4. Select any object on the page. Using **Ancestor** button from properties, choose the **Page** object.

5. Open its **PDF Page Setup** property.

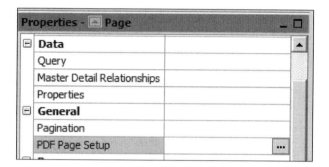

6. Choose the 'Override page setup' option and set the **Orientation** to **Portrait** and size to **A4**.

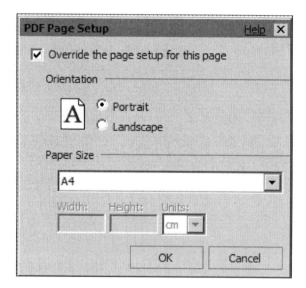

7. Run the report in PDF format and check the output.

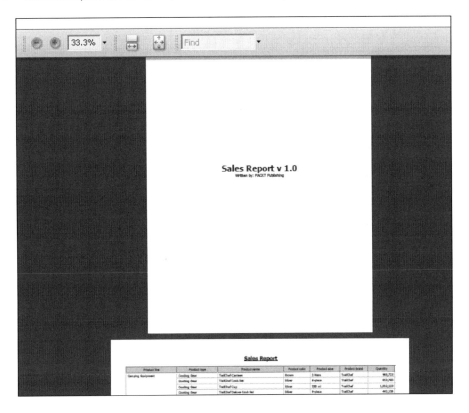

How it works...

This is quite a self-explained, menu-driven functionality. With Cognos 8.3 onwards, it is called **PDF Page Setup**. In earlier versions, it was just called 'Page Setup'.

The sizes and orientations that I have mentioned in the recipe are for example purpose. You should choose the ones that are standard in your organization.

Avoiding page title repetition

The report title defined in Page header is repeated on every page. Business wants it to appear only on the first page. This recipe will show you how to achieve it.

Getting ready

We will use the report created in the previous recipe.

How to do it...

1. We will start by deleting the title from the page header, as this object repeats on every page.

2. Now select the list object and open **List Headers & Footers** dialog from toolbar or menu.

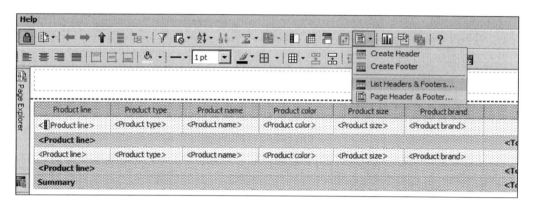

3. Check the option of **Overall header** and click the **OK** button.

4. From properties of the list, define the **Column Titles** as **At start of details**.

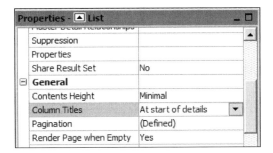

5. Now select the newly added header row from the start of the list. Add the required title to it and define formatting (font size, alignment, and so on).

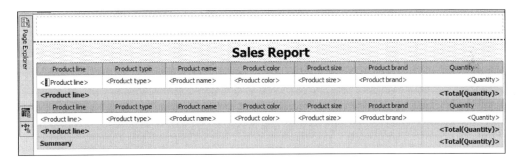

6. Run the report to test it.

How it works...

Anything we add to the page header and page footer is repeated on every page. This consumes space and ink on the PDF output used for printing.

Hence, we use the 'Overall Header' for the list which is shown only once—in the beginning of the list header.

There's more...

The Summary or Grand Total shown for the quantity itself is the 'Overall List Footer' here. Hence, if there are any objects that you would like to show at the end of the report, you need to add one more footer line.

This can be done by adding 'list row cells' below the footer.

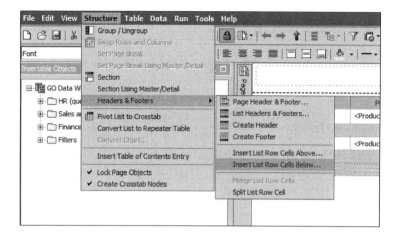

Horizontal pagination

This feature is made available only from version 8.4. It is very useful for printing a very wide report and hence this recipe will show you how to use it.

Earlier Cognos used to fit all report columns in one report width. Hence, in spite of selecting **Landscape** orientation, some very wide reports had to be sized down, leaving them difficult to read. Now, we can choose to span the columns across pages and hence keep the size intact and readable.

Getting ready

We will use the report created in previous recipe for this. In order to mimic that the report can't fit in one page width; we will change the **PDF Page Setup** to the following:

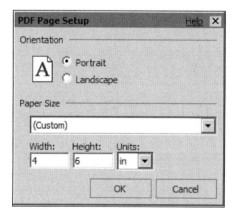

How to do it...

1. Open the report in Report Studio.
2. Select the List object using ancestor button.
3. From properties window, open the pagination dialog.
4. Ensure that the **Allow horizontal pagination** option is checked.

5. Run the report in PDF format to test it.

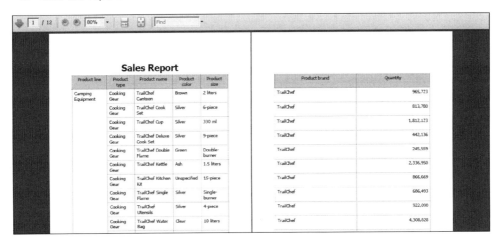

How it works...

This is again a straight forward and menu-driven feature. When a report can't fit in one page width, and if the **Allow horizontal pagination** option is checked, Cognos will span the columns across multiple pages.

They can be then printed and easily referred to side-by-side, which is much better than sizing the contents down and making them unreadable!

There's more...

You can choose a column and define its **Pagination** to **Repeat every page**. That column will then repeat on every page when a report spans many pages horizontally. Columns like **Serial Number** or **Order Number** can be set to this, which will make reading the print-outs (side-by-side) easier.

Choosing output format from prompt

From all of the above recipes, you must have understood now that reports need to be generated in PDF format for printing purpose.

The default output format is HTML which is good for interactive reports with drill-down and drill-throughs. However, it is not printer friendly. They would see one page of output at a time with navigation links at the bottom of the screen, and hence printing the whole report is not straight-forward. For printing, users need to run the report in PDF format. Clicking on the PDF icon resubmits the report query and users have to wait for the execution to finish.

It will be handy to control the report output from prompt page. In this recipe, we will add a prompt control which asks users to specify the output format. This way, users can think of the application (interactive, printing, analysis, and so on) and decide whether the output should be HTML, PDF, Excel, or something else.

Getting ready

We will use the list report created in the previous recipe for this.

How to do it...

1. Open the report in Report Studio.
2. Add a new prompt page to the report from Page Explorer.
3. Open the prompt page and insert a new HTML item in the page body.
4. Define the HTML item as follows:

```
<html>
<head>
<script language="javascript">
function gotoUrl()
{var obj=document.all['OutputFormat'];
/* Below function passed the selected output format to the server
*/
window.onload(gCognosViewer.getRV().viewReport(obj.options[obj.
selectedIndex].value));
```

```
}
 </script>
</head>
<body>
<-- Below will create a dropdown with choices -->
 <select name="OutputFormat" OnBlur="javascript:gotoUrl()">
<option value="HTML">HTML</option>
<option value="PDF">PDF</option>
<option value="singleXLS">Excel 2000 Single Sheet</option>
<option value="spreadsheetML">Excel 2007</option>
<option value="XLWA">Excel 2002</option>
<option value="XLS">Excel 2000</option>
<option value="CSV">Delimited text (CSV)</option>
<option value="XML">XML</option>
</select>
</body>
</html>
```

5. Run the report to test it.

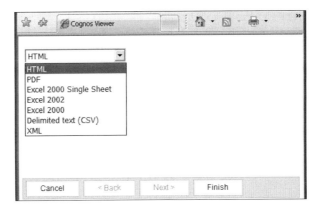

How it works...

This script displayed various output format options in a dropdown. Whatever is selected by the user is passed to the viewer application. This way, we can control the output format from prompt.

There's more...

Instead of giving all the formats as option, you can narrow it down to only HTML, PDF, and Excel. Alternatively, you can also put a checkbox for 'Printable' and if the user selects it, pass the value as PDF or otherwise HTML.

Choosing right colors

Most of the business reports are printed on greyscale printer. This recipe will highlight the importance of choosing the right colors when reports are meant for printing.

Getting ready

We will use the report used in all the previous recipes for this.

How to do it...

1. Open the report in Report Studio. Select the list column titles.
2. From properties, open the **Background Color** dialog. Go to the **Web Safe Colors** tab.
3. Select the #CC99FF color (6th Column, 10th Row).
4. Now select the Product line footer (sub-total) row and set its background color to #CCFF33 (13th Column, 10th Row).

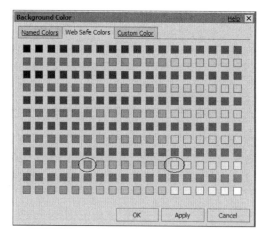

5. Run the report and examine colors. Now print the report and examine colors. You will notice that though both the colors are very different (one is a shade of green and other is purple), they look almost the same on the grayscale printout.
6. Now change the List Column titles to any color from 9th or 11th row. Print the output and you see that the colors are distinguishable now.

How it works...

If you print the whole palette on a grayscale printer, you will notice that rows have alternating light and dark shades. Hence, any two cells from the same row will have very similar output, but those from neighboring rows will have distinguishable shades.

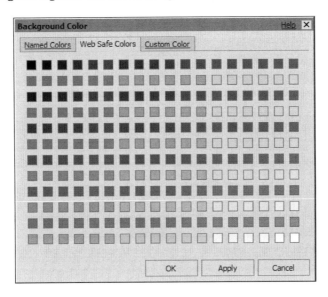

Hence you should always choose one color from an odd numbered row and the other color from an even numbered row.

There's more...

It is good practice to choose a color from a palette than defining custom RGB color. This ensures that the colors can be correctly shown to all output formats.

Defining page set

In a grouped report, it might be sensible to start a new group at a new page. In this recipe, we will see how to achieve it for the Product line grouping.

Getting ready

We will use the report generated in the previous recipe for this.

How to do it...

1. Open the report in Report Studio and go to **Page Explorer**.

2. From Insertable Objects, drag a new **Page Set**.

3. Move the existing report page under this new **Page Set** (within **Detail Pages**).

4. Now select the **Page Set** and from its Properties, set the **Query** to the one being used from report list (that is, **Query1**)

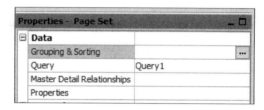

5. Open the **Grouping & Sorting** dialog and drag **Product line** under **Groups**.

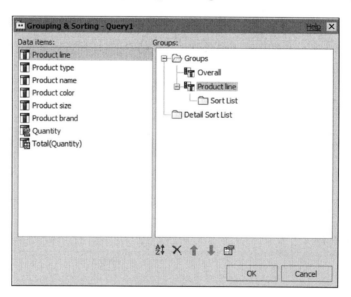

6. Now run the report to test it.

How it works...

When we create Page Set, Cognos generates the report output as a bunch of pages rather than one continuous report. The pages are driven by the query and grouping that we defined in the Page Set properties.

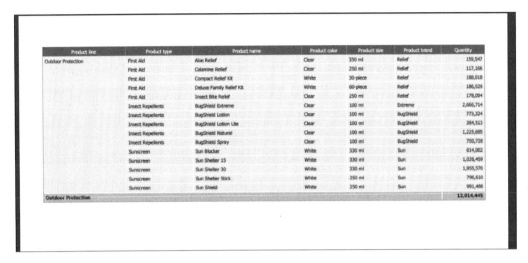

Here, it will create a new page for every Product line. Hence, a new group will start from a new page. This applies to HTML as well as PDF. In Excel, this will create multiple sheets.

Caution about HTML items and JavaScript

This recipe shows you that the HTML items and JavaScripts used on the report page are not executed when report runs in PDF or Excel.

Getting ready

Open the report that we created in Chapter 3, "Generating bar chart with JavaScript" recipe.

How to do it...

1. Run the report in HTML format. Ensure that the bar charts are generated fine.

2. Now re-run the report in PDF format.

3. Notice that bar charts are absent from the PDF output.

How it works...

When users run the report in any format other than HTML, the prompt page generated is still a web page. Hence, any scripts put on the prompt page (for example, default selections) work fine. However, when the actual report is generated, it will execute the scripts only in HTML format.

Hence, the script actions fail in case of PDF, Excel, or any other non-HTML output.

7
Working with Dimensional Models

In this chapter, we will cover the following:

- ▶ List reports or crosstab reports
- ▶ Filtering rows or columns
- ▶ Filtering a whole report
- ▶ Achieving zero suppression
- ▶ Adding a prompt into Slicer and its limitations
- ▶ Level independent MUN for parent-child hierarchy
- ▶ Aggregation versus pre-aggregated values
- ▶ Using the RoleValue function
- ▶ Swapping prompt values while filtering

Introduction

This chapter will discuss some concepts that you should know when developing reports against dimensional or **DMR** (**Dimensionally Modeled Relational**) sources. We will use two packages in this chapter. The "GO Data Warehouse (analysis)" package is of DMR type, whereas 'GO Sales SSAS Cube' is a SQL Server Analysis cube-based package which is purely dimensional in nature.

The GO Data Warehouse (analysis) package comes as a standard sample with Cognos installation and can also be downloaded from the Packt website.

I have created the "GO Sales SSAS Cube package" to connect to the **Microsoft SQL Server Analysis Services** (**SSAS**) cube that comes with the Cognos sample installation. You can also use other sample cubes (Essbase or Powercube). You can download this package from the Packt website or even easily create one.

List report or crosstab report

This recipe shows that most of the times it is possible to use a crosstab report instead of a list report, and then discusses the pros and cons of each.

Getting ready

We will use the "GO Data Warehouse (analysis)" package for this.

How to do it...

1. Create a new **List** type of report based on this package.

2. Drag columns on the list shown as follows. Create grouping and sorting for **Product line** and **Product**.

Product line	Product	Quantity	Unit cost	Unit price	Unit sale price	Gross margin	Revenue	Gross profit	Product cost	Planned revenue
<Product line>	<Product>	<Quantity>	<Unit cost>	<Unit price>	<Unit sale price>	<Gross margin>	<Revenue>	<Gross profit>	<Product cost>	<Planned revenue>
	<Product>	<Quantity>	<Unit cost>	<Unit price>	<Unit sale price>	<Gross margin>	<Revenue>	<Gross profit>	<Product cost>	<Planned revenue>
<Product line>	<Product>	<Quantity>	<Unit cost>	<Unit price>	<Unit sale price>	<Gross margin>	<Revenue>	<Gross profit>	<Product cost>	<Planned revenue>
	<Product>	<Quantity>	<Unit cost>	<Unit price>	<Unit sale price>	<Gross margin>	<Revenue>	<Gross profit>	<Product cost>	<Planned revenue>

3. Run the report to test it.

4. Now save this report and create a new report of 'Crosstab' type.

5. Drag items on the crosstab shown as follows. Define sorting on **Product line** and **Product**.

		<#Quantity#>	<#Unit cost#>	<#Unit price#>	<#Unit sale price#>	<#Gross margin#>	<#Revenue#>	<#Gross profit#>	<#Product cost#>	<#Planned revenue#>
<#Product line#>	<#Product#>	<#1234#>	<#1234#>	<#1234#>	<#1234#>	<#1234#>	<#1234#>	<#1234#>	<#1234#>	<#1234#>
	<#Product#>	<#1234#>	<#1234#>	<#1234#>	<#1234#>	<#1234#>	<#1234#>	<#1234#>	<#1234#>	<#1234#>
<#Product line#>	<#Product#>	<#1234#>	<#1234#>	<#1234#>	<#1234#>	<#1234#>	<#1234#>	<#1234#>	<#1234#>	<#1234#>
	<#Product#>	<#1234#>	<#1234#>	<#1234#>	<#1234#>	<#1234#>	<#1234#>	<#1234#>	<#1234#>	<#1234#>

6. Run the report to test it.

How it works...

You will see that both reports bring the same data back. It is a general practice to use lists for relational models whereas crosstabs for dimensional models. I believe this practice comes from the fact that multidimensional databases (cubes) are accessed using MDX that naturally returns the data in two axes.

However, the biggest factors that drive the choice as per my opinion are:

1. Dynamicity of columns.
2. Number oriented or text oriented.
3. Report access method (HTML or not).

When the number of columns and column members are dynamic in nature and driven by values from a dimension or query subject, you need to use crosstab.

Crosstab reports can show only numbers in the intersections. The textual fields need to be on rows or columns. Hence, if you need to show more textual information, you should use list report rather than pulling them all as nested rows which will deteriorate the performance.

List reports are better for interactive (HTML) output. As soon as Cognos receives the top 20 (or whatever is the setting) rows, the first page is displayed to the users. Hence, it reduces the wait time. With crosstab, more often than not, Cognos waits for full data before showing even the first page.

Hence, not just the data source type, but all these factors should be considered before taking the decision.

Filtering rows or columns

This recipe will show you how to filter row or column members in a crosstab report.

Getting ready

This report will be based on the dimensional source. Hence, please use the "GO Sales SSAS cube" package which connects to the GO Sales cube for this recipe.

How to do it...

1. Create a new crosstab report.

2. Drag **Current Year** and **Current Month** on columns; and **Organization Code 2** level on rows. Drag **Stmt Year** measure in the intersection.

Stmt Year	<#Current Year#>		<#Current Year#>	
	<#Current Month#>	<#Current Month#>	<#Current Month#>	<#Current Month#>
<#Organization Code2#>	<#1234#>	<#1234#>	<#1234#>	<#1234#>
<#Organization Code2#>	<#1234#>	<#1234#>	<#1234#>	<#1234#>

3. Run the report to test it. The report will look like this.

Stmt Year	2004				
	Opening balance Opening balance 2004	1 January 2004	2 February 2004	3 March 2004	4 April 2004
000					
Eliminations					
GO Accessories Inc.	1,274,831,095.96	-94,957,114.68	-109,343,701.08	-96,203,238.52	-101,457,893.68
GOCCP					
GOCON					
Great Outdoors Company - Americas	4,110,376,337.64	-8,066,933.00	-18,142,616.24	-4,536,297.48	-2,933,430.00
Great Outdoors Company - Asia Pacific	33,418,949,756.73	0.00	0.00	0.00	0.00

4. Now we will try to filter the rows such that only those Organization Codes are displayed which have data. For that delete **Organization Code 2** from rows.

5. Drag a new **Set Expression** on rows.

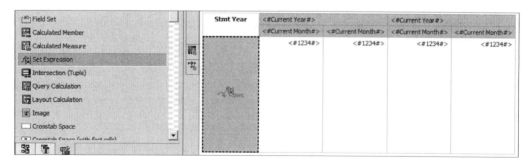

6. Call this set as **Filtered Org** and base it on **Organization Dim**.

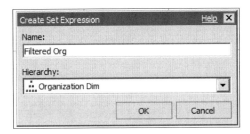

7. Define the set expression as: filter([GO Finance Fact].[Organization Dim].[Organization Dim].[Organization Code2], [Stmt Year] is not null).

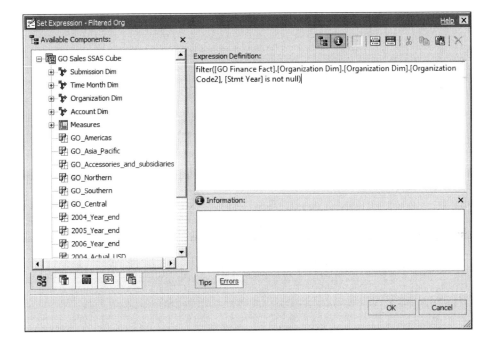

8. Now run the report to test it.

Stmt Year	2004				
	Opening balance Opening balance 2004	1 January 2004	2 February 2004	3 March 2004	4 April 2004
GO Accessories Inc.	1,274,831,095.96	-94,957,114.6799998	-109,343,701.079999	-96,203,238.52	-101,457,893.68
Great Outdoors Company - Americas	4,110,376,337.64	-8,066,933	-18,142,616.2399988	-4,536,297.47999954	-2,933,430
Great Outdoors Company - Asia Pacific	33,418,949,756.73	0	0	-0.00000763	0.00001526

How it works...

The Report Studio filters (summary and detail) are useful mainly with relational data sources and list reports. With cube based reports, you can achieve better performance by filtering the row and column members beforehand in the expression that pulls the members.

Here we use the filter function which allows us to define the criteria. Criteria can be based on the member properties or measures. We used it for zero rows suppression; hence we filtered on the required measure. However, you can also filter on member properties, caption, keys, and so on. It is a common practice to have certain flags or categories as member properties which can then be used for filtering depending on user selection.

There's more...

If you are using Cognos version 8.4, you can use the ready functionality to suppress the zero rows and columns. Please refer to the "Achieving zero suppression" recipe for details.

This recipe teaches you a general concept of filtering out the members on rows and columns which you can use for many criteria in addition to zero suppression

Filtering whole report

This recipe will show you how to filter the values of whole report based on a data item that does not appear on the report. We will filter the report created in the previous recipe to show values for a selected "Balance sheet" account.

Getting ready

We will use the report created in the previous recipe for this.

How to do it...

1. Open the report in Report Studio.

2. Go to **Query Explorer** and open the query used by the crosstab on report page.

3. From **Insertable Objects** pane, browse the cube for required member. Here we will search for **Assets (total)** from the **Balance sheet** hierarchy.

4. After locating the member, drag it on the query under slicer.

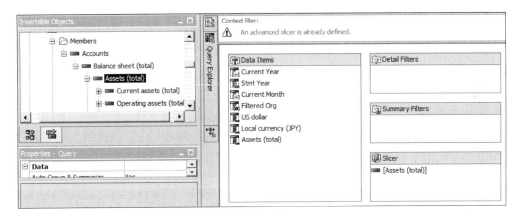

5. Run the report to test it.

How it works...

When you want to define a context for the values, or filter the values based on a dimension which does not appear on the report, you can use **Slicer**.

You can drag a member or set of members under Slicer. This defines the overall context for the query and all the numbers in the crosstab are filtered for that member or set of members. Again, use of Slicer goes naturally with the way multi-dimensional databases are accessed. Using a summary or detailed filtered instead of Slicer is possible but not advisable.

There's more...

You can make the Slicer member/member set dynamic, so that users can select a value for it from the prompt. This is covered in the next recipe.

Adding prompt into slicer and its limitation

In the previous recipe, we saw that we can filter the whole report by a member or member set, using Slicer. This recipe will show you how to add a prompt into Slicer to make it dynamic.

Getting ready

Create a simple crosstab report with **Organization Code 2** on rows and **Current Year** and **Current Months** on columns.

How to do it...

1. Open the **Query Explorer** and explore the query being used by crosstab.

2. From **Insertable Objects** pane, drag a new **Set Expression** under Slicer.

3. Define the set as: `[GO Finance Fact].[Submission Dim].[Submission Dim].[Submission Currency En]->?SubmissionCcy?`.

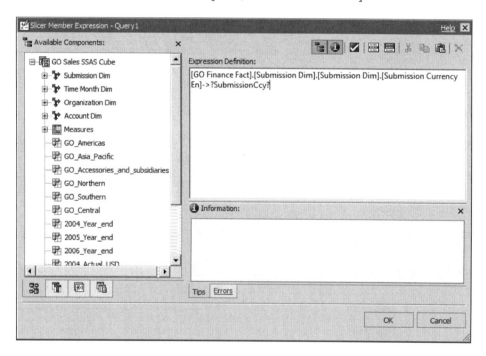

4. Run the report to test it.

How it works...

When you run the report, you will set the Cognos to automatically prompt you to select a Submission Currency. When you select one, the report runs and pulls data for selected Submission Currency.

Here, we are using Slicer for the same application as in the previous recipe. However, instead of hard-coding a particular member, we are making it prompt driven. The first part of the expression (before this pointer - >) defines the hierarchy. The second part is the parameter name which is dynamically replaced by Member Unique Name based on your selection.

There's more...

You will notice that you can select only value for Submission Currency. This is because the expression expects only one member. However, it is possible to make it multi-select. For that, put the expression within the set () function.

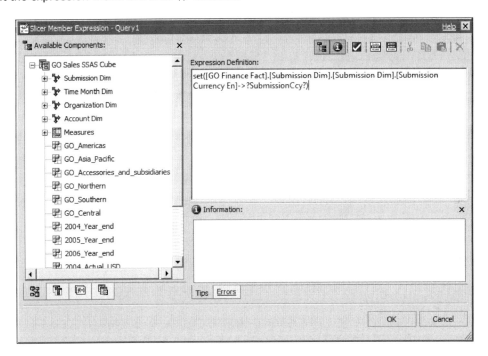

Now when you run the report, you will be prompted for Submission Currency and you will be able to select more than one currency.

It is good practice to define your own prompt on the prompt page instead of letting Cognos generate the prompt at run-time. That way you can have control on the appearance, ordering, and performance of prompt page.

More Info

The biggest issue with Slicer is that you cannot make it **Optional**. It works like a mandatory filter. There is a workaround to this which involves using the Prompt Macro. However, that adds complexity to the code and sometimes I have seen other problems cropping up after using the Prompt Macro for this.

Hence, if you need to have optional filter, you might decide to go with the traditional detail filters where you can set the **Usage property**.

New feature for zero suppression

We have already seen one way of suppressing zero rows in the "Filtering rows or columns" recipe. This recipe will show you the new feature introduced in version 8.4 for the same.

Getting ready

We will use the same 'GO Sales SSAS cube' package for this.

How to do it...

1. Create a simple list report with **Organization Code2** on rows, and **Current Year** and **Current Month** on columns.

2. Now select anything on the crosstab and using **Ancestor** button from **Properties** tab, select the crosstab.

3. Open its **Suppression** property.

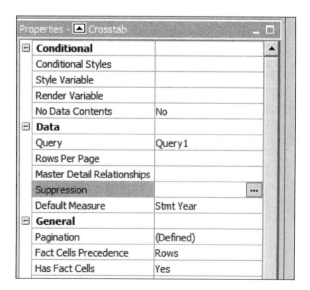

4. Select the **Rows only** option for **Suppression** and keep the appropriate
    checkboxes checked.

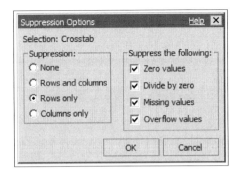

5. Run the report to test it.

How it works...

When you run the report, you will see that only those organization codes appear on the rows
which have some data. This effect is same as the filtering we had achieved by using the
calculated member set.

I would say this is one of the most useful feature introduced in version 8.4. You can choose
to suppress only rows, only columns, both or none. Also, you can choose whether you want to
suppress zeros, divide by zero, missing values, or overflow values.

There's more...

If there is only one data container on the report, you can set the suppression options from the
menu also. For that, go to **Data | Suppress** and choose appropriate option.

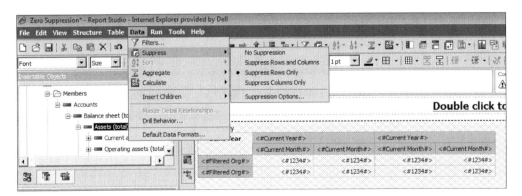

You can also use the **Suppress** icon from toolbar.

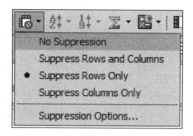

Level independent MUN for parent child hierarchy

Some multi-dimensional databases provide facility to define parent-child hierarchy. I believe this is one of the strongest features of MSAS cube. This recipe will talk about the Member Unique Name for a member from parent-child hierarchy and how to make it level independent.

Please note that the feature of parent-child hierarchy is not available in PowerPlay. So if you are using the PowerPlay cube for practice, you won't be able to perform this recipe.

Getting ready

Create a simple crosstab report with **Organization Code2** on rows and **Current Year** on columns. Drag **Stmt Year** in the intersection.

How to do it...

1. We will first add a member from parent-child hierarchy on the report. GO Sales cube comes with 'Account Dim' dimension which is of the parent-child type.

    First of all, from the menu bar, choose **Tool | Options**. From the **Report** tab, uncheck the option **Alias member unique names**.

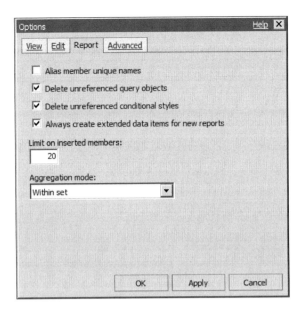

2. Now, open the crosstab query from query explorer and drag **Accounts receivable – net** member under Slicer. (This is similar to "Filtering whole report" recipe).

3. Now double-click on this Slicer item and examine the expression.

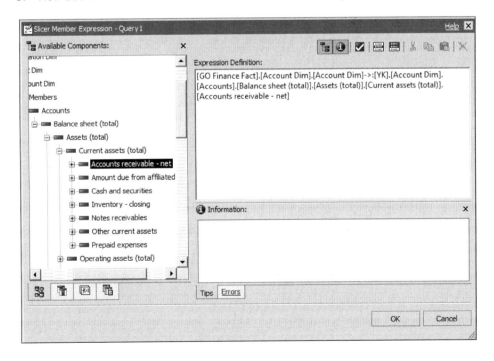

4. You will notice that this MUN has reference to the parents of **Account receivable – net**. This makes it dependant on the level.

5. Replace the expression with this one: `[GO Finance Fact].[Account Dim].`
`[Account Dim]->:[YK].[Account Dim].[Accounts receivable - net].`

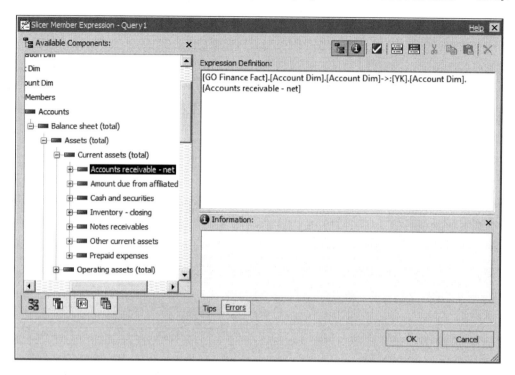

6. Run the report to test it. The report should still work the same with the member now not referring to the fixed parents.

How it works...

The basic aim of any parent-child hierarchy is to maintain the flexibility of structure. The members can move up, down, and across very easily without breaking the overall tree.

However, when any member from such hierarchy is dragged on the report, Cognos actually remembers what level it comes from. This hampers the flexibility and in future if the member moves under another parent, the report will stop working.

Here, we solve that issue by removing the references to levels. We retain the first part of MUN which tells which hierarchy to refer to. However, from second part, we only keep the hierarchy name and the member key. This is sufficient to identify the member from the hierarchy and also keeps it flexible.

Aggregation versus pre-aggregated values

The biggest advantage of using a cube as data source is its capability to pre-aggregate values. This recipe will show you how to exploit this feature of cube in your Cognos reports.

Getting ready

Create a simple crosstab report using **GO Sales SSAS Cube** package. Pull **Organization Code2** and **Code3** on rows, and **Current Year** on columns. Drag **Stmt Year** in the intersection.

How to do it...

1. First, we will create aggregation using standard method. For that, select the **Organization Code3** row.

2. From the toolbar, click on the **Aggregate** button and choose **Aggregate**.

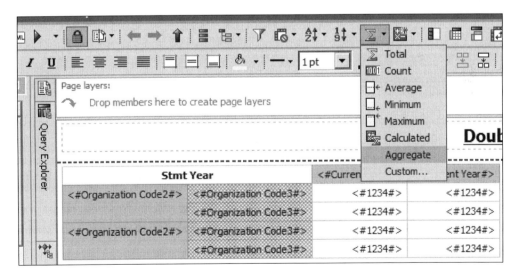

3. Run the report to test it.

Stmt Year		2004	2005	2006	2007
GO Accessories Inc.	Great Outdoors Company - Northern Europe	344,705,572	263,636	-42,251,058	0
	GOEUX - Corporate Divisions	472,228,481	497,950,414	517,434,754	193,086,354
	GOEUX - Operations	-876,248,412	-364,003,472	-698,935,260	-193,086,354
	Great Outdoors Company - Central Europe	359,421,142	18,830,252	-607,456	-431,771
	Great Outdoors Company - Southern Europe	270,964,457	92,969,818	-72,170,164	-74,545
	Aggregate(Organization Code3)	**571,071,241**	**246,010,649**	**-296,529,184**	**-506,317**
Great Outdoors Company - Americas	GOAMX - Corporate Divisions	5,175,165,570	5,450,344,776	5,591,077,517	2,117,607,458
	GOAMX - Operations	-1,236,339,728	-5,966,734,372	-8,557,760,131	-4,148,910,425
	Aggregate(Organization Code3)	**3,938,825,843**	**-516,389,596**	**-2,966,682,614**	**-2,031,302,967**
Great Outdoors Company - Asia Pacific	GOEAX - Corporate Divisions	35,348,222,906	37,248,048,608	38,753,630,284	14,457,830,038
	GOEAX - Operations	-1,929,273,149	-37,785,277,295	-38,753,630,284	-14,457,830,038
	Aggregate(Organization Code3)	**33,418,949,757**	**-537,228,687**	**0**	**0**

4. Now go back to the Report Studio. Delete the new row created for **Aggregation**.

5. Go to second tab (Data Item) of Insertable objects. Drag **Organization Code2** again on report and drop it under **Organization Code3** and format this row to be bold; shown as follows:

Stmt Year		<#Current Year#>	<#Current Year#>
<#Organization Code2#>	<#Organization Code3#>	<#1234#>	<#1234#>
	<#Organization Code2#>	**<#1234#>**	**<#1234#>**
<#Organization Code2#>	<#Organization Code3#>	<#1234#>	<#1234#>
	<#Organization Code2#>	**<#1234#>**	**<#1234#>**

6. Now run the report to test it.

Stmt Year		2004	2005	2006	2007
GO Accessories Inc.	Great Outdoors Company - Northern Europe	344,705,572	263,636	-42,251,058	0
	GOEUX - Corporate Divisions	472,228,481	497,950,414	517,434,754	193,086,354
	GOEUX - Operations	-876,248,412	-364,003,472	-698,935,260	-193,086,354
	Great Outdoors Company - Central Europe	359,421,142	18,830,252	-607,456	-431,771
	Great Outdoors Company - Southern Europe	270,964,457	92,969,818	-72,170,164	-74,545
	GO Accessories Inc.	**571,071,241**	**246,010,649**	**-296,529,184**	**-506,317**
Great Outdoors Company - Americas	GOAMX - Corporate Divisions	5,175,165,570	5,450,344,776	5,591,077,517	2,117,607,458
	GOAMX - Operations	-1,236,339,728	-5,966,734,372	-8,557,760,131	-4,148,910,425
	Great Outdoors Company - Americas	**3,938,825,843**	**-516,389,596**	**-2,966,682,614**	**-2,031,302,967**
Great Outdoors Company - Asia Pacific	GOEAX - Corporate Divisions	35,348,222,906	37,248,048,608	38,753,630,284	14,457,830,038
	GOEAX - Operations	-1,929,273,149	-37,785,277,295	-38,753,630,284	-14,457,830,038
	Great Outdoors Company - Asia Pacific	**33,418,949,757**	**-537,228,687**	**0**	**0**

7. Notice that the aggregated values are the same.

How it works...

The first method that we used to create aggregation rows, utilizes the Cognos's aggregation feature. That is a standard way in case of relational data sources. However, Cognos won't use the pre-aggregated values from the cube in that case. Instead, it will calculate the aggregations at run time either locally or at the database.

In order to utilize the pre-aggregation feature of cube, we then dragged the item Organization Code3 under Organization Code2. That way, we make Report Studio ask for the pre-aggregated values from the cube.

We can test that the values coming in the report from both approaches are same and correct. The latter one is a good practice when writing report against cubes. It dramatically improves the performance of the report.

There's more...

In the first approach, the aggregation row title is a static text. Whereas, in the second approach, the aggregation row titles change dynamically to show the **Organization Code2**.

Either way, you can control this by editing the **Source Type** property of the row title.

RoleValue() function

This recipe will show you a useful function which you will often need while working with dimensional and dimensionally-modeled-relational models.

As the purpose of this recipe is only to examine this function, we won't consider any specific business case here.

Getting ready

Create a new list type of report based on the same **GO Sales SSAS Cube** package.

How to do it...

1. From **Insertable Objects**, locate **Organization Code2**.

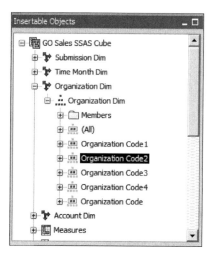

2. Drag it on the list as a new column.

3. Now add a new data item to the list. Define it as:
   ```
   roleValue('_businessKey',[Organization Code2]).
   ```

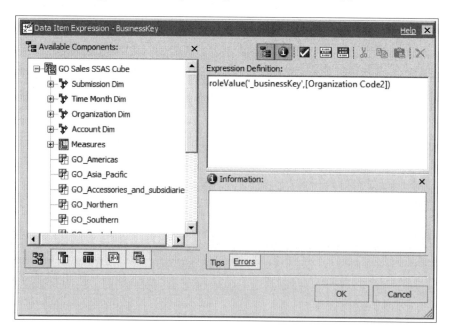

4. Add two more data items and define them as follows:

```
roleValue('_memberCaption',[Organization Code2])
roleValue('_memberUniqueName',[Organization Code2])
```

5. Run the report to test it.

RoleValue function

Organization Code2	BusinessKey	Caption	MUN
000	000	000	[GO Finance Fact].[Organization Dim].[Organization Dim].[Organization Code2]->:[YK].[Organization Dim].[Organization Dim].[Great Outdoors Consolidated Inc.].[000]
Eliminations	GOCEL	Eliminations	[GO Finance Fact].[Organization Dim].[Organization Dim].[Organization Code2]->:[YK].[Organization Dim].[Organization Dim].[Great Outdoors Consolidated Inc.].[Eliminations]
GO Accessories Inc.	GOEUX	GO Accessories Inc.	[GO Finance Fact].[Organization Dim].[Organization Dim].[Organization Code2]->:[YK].[Organization Dim].[Organization Dim].[Great Outdoors Consolidated Inc.].[GO Accessories Inc.]
GOCCP	GOCCP	GOCCP	[GO Finance Fact].[Organization Dim].[Organization Dim].[Organization Code2]->:[YK].[Organization Dim].[Organization Dim].[Great Outdoors Consolidated Inc.].[GOCCP]

How it works...

When defining a **DMR (Dimensionally Modeled Relational)** model in Framework Manager, the modeler can define various columns as attributes. This `roleValue()` function allows you to access these attributes.

This function takes two arguments: Role and Member/Set.

In case of MSAS cube, we can't define custom attributes in FM. However, we can still use this function to access intrinsic roles: `_businessKey, _memberCaption, _memberDescription, _memberUniqueName`. In this recipe, we checked some of these intrinsic roles.

Swapping dimensions using string manipulation

When a prompt is based on a dimension, the selected value is passed as a full qualifier (**Member Unique Name**), not just the key. This results in limitation of the prompt use. We cannot use the prompt to filter any other dimension.

In this recipe, we will see how to over-ride this limitation by doing the string manipulation of MUN.

Consider a business case where the cube has two time dimensions (say Billing date and Transaction date). Users want a choice on prompt page to select which time dimension to filter on. Also, they will select a Date (Year or Month) on the prompt page, and we need to filter the appropriate time dimension.

Getting ready

I added a role playing dimension to the GO Sales cube for this. This is called 'Transaction Time Month'. Ideally, it should join to the fact based on a different key than the pre-existing 'Time Month Dim'. However, this being just for illustration, I have used the same key.

You can download this cube from the Packt website or you can choose to design one yourself after reading this recipe.

How to do it...

1. Firstly, we will add a value prompt (radio button) on the prompt page with static choices for **Time Period Dim** and **Transaction Period**.

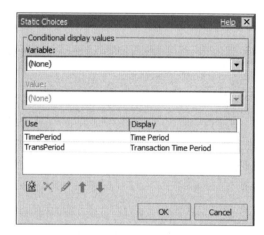

2. Now add a new conditional variable to link to this radio button prompt.

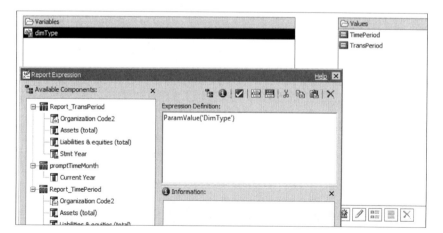

3. On the report page, add a conditional block and link it to the **DimType** variable defined above as Block Variable.

4. Set Current Block to **TimePeriod** and add a crosstab to the block. Drag valid members on the crosstab as shown. Also, add a text saying **Sliced on Time Period dimension**.

5. Now set Current Block to **TransPeriod** and add a new crosstab to the block. Drag appropriate members on the crosstab and add a text saying **Sliced on Transaction Period dimension**.

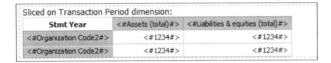

6. By now we have achieved a report that will show one of the two crosstabs depending on the choice selected by user on radio button prompt. Now we will add the time period prompt.

7. For that, go to the prompt page and add a tree prompt based on **Transaction Time Month** dimension. Call the parameter as **TimeMonth**.

8. Now go to the query that drives the **Transaction Time** crosstab. Add a slicer as: [GO Finance Fact].[Transaction Time Month].[Transaction Time Month. Time Month Dim].[Current Year]->?TimeMonth?

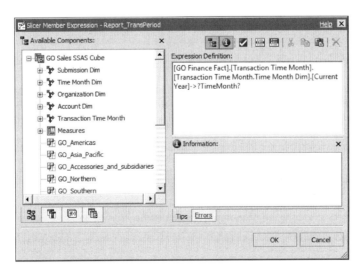

9. Finally go to the query that drives the **Time Period** crosstab. Add a slicer
    as: #substitute('Transaction Time Month','Time Month
    Dim',substitute('Transaction Time Month','Time Month Dim','[GO
    Finance Fact].[Transaction Time Month].[Transaction Time Month.
    Time Month Dim].[Current Year]->?TimeMonth?')   )#

10. Now run the report to test it. You will see that report shows appropriate crosstab
    depending on the selection, and both crosstabs filter data on different
    dimension—though the prompt is based only on one dimension.

How it works...

The Substitute function is a macro function to do literal replacements. It looks for the first
occurrence of mentioned string (Transaction Time Month) and replaces it with the
substitution string (Time Month Dim). As we need to replace both the occurrences, we
need to use the Substitute() function twice. Hence, we successfully changed the Member
Unique Name of the selected **Transaction Time Month** member to refer to the same member
in **Time Month Dim** hierarchy.

Though this recipe is very lengthy, the basic principle it shows here is – manipulating the MUN
using macros. We are using the substitute function to do appropriate string replacements
and achieve the desired MUN. We retain the KEY of the member and just change the
preceding qualifier.

You can build upon this idea to achieve many sophisticated functionalities in the reports.

See also

To learn more about the slicers and adding prompts to slicers, please refer to earlier recipes
of this chapter.

Macros will be discussed in more detail in next chapter, which is called *Macros*.

8
Macros

In this chapter, we will cover the following:

- ▶ Add data level security using CSVIdentityMap macro
- ▶ Using prompt macros in native SQL
- ▶ Making prompts optional
- ▶ Adding a token macro
- ▶ Using prompt and PromptMany macros in query subjects
- ▶ Showing the prompts in a report based on security
- ▶ String operations to get it right
- ▶ Showing a user name in the footer

Introduction

This chapter will introduce you to an interesting and useful tool of Cognos BI, called 'macros'. They can be used in Framework Manager as well as Report Studio. In this book, we are not covering Framework Manager, hence I will restrict myself to the use of macros in Report Studio.

The Cognos engine understands the presence of a macro as it is written within a pair of hashes (#). It executes the macros first and puts the result back into report specification like a literal string replacement. We can use this to alter data items, filters, and slicers at run time.

You won't find the macro functions and their details within Report Studio environment (which is strange, as it fully supports them). Anyways, you can always open Framework Manager and check different macro functions and their syntaxes from there. Also, there is documentation available in Cognos' help and online materials.

We have already seen one example of macros in *Chapter 7, Working with Dimensional Model* (in the"Swapping dimension" recipe). In this chapter, I will show you more examples and introduce you to more functions which you can later build upon to achieve sophisticated functionalities.

We will be writing some SQL straight against the GO Data Warehouse data source. Also, we will use the "GO Data Warehouse (Query)" package for some recipes.

Add data level security using CSVIdentityMap macro

A report shows the employee names by region and country. We need to implement data security in this report such that a user can see the records only for the country he belongs to. There are already **User Groups** defined on the Cognos server (in the directory) and users are made members of appropriate groups.

For this sample, I have added my user account to a user group called 'Spain'.

Getting ready

Open a new list report with **GO Data Warehouse (Query)** as the package.

How to do it...

1. Drag the appropriate columns (**Region**, **Country**, and **Employee name**) on to the report from **Employee by Region** query subject.

Region	Country	Employee name
<Region>	<Country>	<Employee name>
<Region>	<Country>	<Employee name>
<Region>	<Country>	<Employee name>

2. Go to **Query Explorer** and drag a new detail filter.
3. Define the filter as: `[Country] in (#CSVIdentityNameList(',')#)`

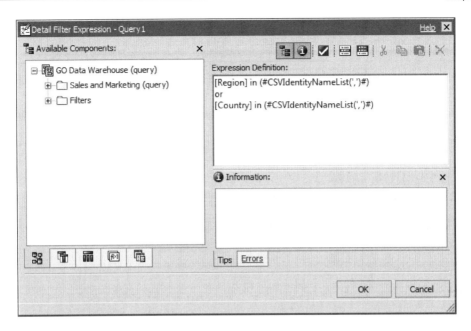

4. Run the report to test it. You will notice that a user can see only the rows of the country/countries of which he is a member.

How it works...

Here we are using a macro function called `CSVIdentityNameList`. This function returns a list of groups and roles that the user belongs to, along with the user's account name. Hence, when I run the report, one of the values returned will be 'Spain' and I will see data for Spain.

The function accepts a string parameter which is used as a separator in the result. Here we are passing a comma (,) as the separator.

If a user belongs to multiple country groups, he will see data for all the countries listed in the result of a macro.

There's more...

This solution, conspicuously, has its limitations. None of the user accounts or roles should be same as a country name, because that will wrongly show data for a country the user does not belong to. For example, for a user called 'Paris', it will show data for the 'Paris' region. So, there need to be certain restrictions. However, you can build upon the knowledge of this macro function and use it in many practical business scenarios.

Using prompt macro in native SQL

In this recipe, we will write an SQL statement straight to be fired on the data source. We will use the Prompt macro to dynamically change the filter condition.

We will write a report that shows list of employee by Region and Country. We will use the Prompt macro to ask the users to enter a country name. Then the SQL statement will search for the employee belonging to that country.

Getting ready

Create a new blank list report against 'GO Data Warehouse (Query)' package.

How to do it...

1. Go to the **Query Explorer** and drag an **SQL** object on the Query Subject that is linked to the list (**Query1** in usual case).

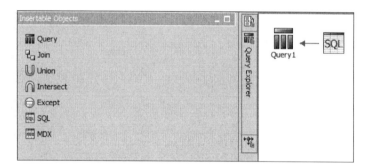

2. Select the **SQL** object and ensure that `great_outdoor_warehouse` is selected as the data source.

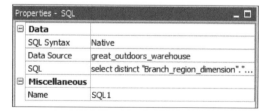

3. Open the SQL property and add the following statement:

```
select distinct "Branch_region_dimension"."REGION_EN" "Region" ,
"Branch_region_dimension"."COUNTRY_EN" "Country" , "EMP_EMPLOYEE_
DIM"."EMPLOYEE_NAME" "Employee_name"
```

```
from "GOSALESDW"."GO_REGION_DIM" "Branch_region_dimension",
"GOSALESDW"."EMP_EMPLOYEE_DIM" "EMP_EMPLOYEE_DIM",
"GOSALESDW"."GO_BRANCH_DIM" "GO_BRANCH_DIM"
where ("Branch_region_dimension"."COUNTRY_EN" in
(#prompt('Region')#))
and "Branch_region_dimension"."COUNTRY_CODE" = "GO_BRANCH_
DIM"."COUNTRY_CODE" and "EMP_EMPLOYEE_DIM"."BRANCH_CODE" = "GO_
BRANCH_DIM"."BRANCH_CODE"
```

4. Hit the **OK** button. This will validate the query and will close the dialog box. You will see that three data items (`Region`, `Country`, and `Employee_Name`) are added to **Query1**.

5. Now go to the report page. Drag these data items on the list and run the report to test it.

How it works...

Here we are using the macro in native SQL statement. Native SQL allows us to directly fire a query on the data source and use the result on the report. This is useful in certain scenarios where we don't need to define any Framework Model. If you examine the SQL statement, you will notice that it is a very simple one that joins three tables and returns appropriate columns. We have added a filter condition on country name which is supposed to dynamically change depending on the value entered by user.

The macro function that we have used here is `Prompt()`. As the name suggests, it is used to generate a prompt and returns the parameter value back to be used in an SQL statement.

`Prompt()` function takes five arguments. The first argument is the parameter name and it is mandatory. It allows us to link a prompt page object (value prompt, date prompt, and so on) to the prompt function. The rest of the four arguments are optional and we are not using them here. You will read about them in the next recipe.

 Please note that we also have an option of adding a detail filter in the query subject instead of using `PROMPT()` macro within query. However, sometimes you would want to filter a table before joining it with other tables. In that case, using `PROMPT()` macro within the query helps.

There's more...

Similar to the `Prompt()` function, there is a `PromptMany()` macro function. This works in exactly the same way and allows users to enter multiple values for the parameter. Those values are returned as a comma-separated list.

Making prompt optional

The previous recipe showed you how to generate a prompt through a macro. In this recipe, we will see how to make it optional using other arguments of the function.

We will generate two simple list reports, both based on a native SQL. These lists will show product details for selected product line. However, the product line prompt will be made optional using two different approaches.

Getting ready

Create a report with two simple list objects based on native SQL. For that, create the Query Subjects in the same way as we did in the previous recipe. Use the following query in the SQL objects:

```
select distinct "SLS_PRODUCT_LINE_LOOKUP"."PRODUCT_LINE_EN" "Product_
line" , "SLS_PRODUCT_LOOKUP"."PRODUCT_NAME" "Product_name" , "SLS_
PRODUCT_COLOR_LOOKUP"."PRODUCT_COLOR_EN" "Product_color" , "SLS_
PRODUCT_SIZE_LOOKUP"."PRODUCT_SIZE_EN" "Product_size"
 from "GOSALESDW"."SLS_PRODUCT_DIM" "SLS_PRODUCT_DIM",
"GOSALESDW"."SLS_PRODUCT_LINE_LOOKUP" "SLS_PRODUCT_LINE_LOOKUP",
"GOSALESDW"."SLS_PRODUCT_TYPE_LOOKUP" "SLS_PRODUCT_TYPE_
LOOKUP", "GOSALESDW"."SLS_PRODUCT_LOOKUP" "SLS_PRODUCT_LOOKUP",
"GOSALESDW"."SLS_PRODUCT_COLOR_LOOKUP" "SLS_PRODUCT_COLOR_LOOKUP",
"GOSALESDW"."SLS_PRODUCT_SIZE_LOOKUP" "SLS_PRODUCT_SIZE_LOOKUP",
"GOSALESDW"."SLS_PRODUCT_BRAND_LOOKUP" "SLS_PRODUCT_BRAND_LOOKUP"
 where "SLS_PRODUCT_LOOKUP"."PRODUCT_LANGUAGE" = N'EN' and "SLS_
PRODUCT_DIM"."PRODUCT_LINE_CODE" = "SLS_PRODUCT_LINE_LOOKUP"."PRODUCT_
LINE_CODE" and "SLS_PRODUCT_DIM"."PRODUCT_NUMBER" = "SLS_PRODUCT_
LOOKUP"."PRODUCT_NUMBER" and "SLS_PRODUCT_DIM"."PRODUCT_SIZE_CODE"
= "SLS_PRODUCT_SIZE_LOOKUP"."PRODUCT_SIZE_CODE" and "SLS_PRODUCT_
DIM"."PRODUCT_TYPE_CODE" = "SLS_PRODUCT_TYPE_LOOKUP"."PRODUCT_TYPE_
CODE" and "SLS_PRODUCT_DIM"."PRODUCT_COLOR_CODE" = "SLS_PRODUCT_COLOR_
LOOKUP"."PRODUCT_COLOR_CODE" and "SLS_PRODUCT_BRAND_LOOKUP"."PRODUCT_
BRAND_CODE" = "SLS_PRODUCT_DIM"."PRODUCT_BRAND_CODE"
```

This is a simple query that joins product related tables and retrieves required columns.

How to do it...

1. We have created two list reports based on two SQL query subjects. Both the SQL objects use the same query as mentioned above. Now, we will start with altering them. For that open **Query Explorer**. Rename first query subject as **Optional_defaultValue** and the second one as **Pure_Optional**.

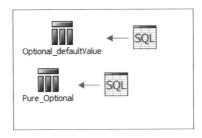

2. In the `Optional_defaultValue` SQL object, amend the query with following lines:

   ```
   and
   "SLS_PRODUCT_LINE_LOOKUP"."PRODUCT_LINE_EN" = #sq(prompt ('Product
   Line','string','Golf Equipment'))#
   ```

3. Similarly, amend the `Pure_Optional` SQL object query with the following line:

   ```
   #prompt ('Product Line','string','and 1=1', ' and "SLS_PRODUCT_
   LINE_LOOKUP"."PRODUCT_LINE_EN" = ')#
   ```

4. Now run the report. You will be prompted to enter a product line. Don't enter any value and just hit **OK** button. Notice that the report runs (which means the prompt is optional). First, list object returns rows for 'Golf Equipment'. The second list is populated by all the products.

How it works...

Fundamentally, this report works the same as the one in the previous report. We are firing the SQL statements straight on the data source. The filter condition in the WHERE clause are using the PROMPT macro.

Optional_defaultValue

In this query, we are using the second and third arguments of Prompt () function. Second argument defines the data type of value which is 'String' in our case. The third argument defines default value of the prompt. When the user doesn't enter any value for the prompt, this default value is used. This is what makes the prompt optional. As we have defined 'Golf Equipment' as the default value, the first list object shows data for 'Golf Equipment' when prompt is left unfilled.

Pure_Optional

In this query, we are using fourth argument of Prompt () function. This argument is of string type. If the user provides any value for the prompt, the prompt value is concatenated to this string argument and the result is returned.

In our case, the fourth argument is the left part of filtering condition that is, `'and "SLS_PRODUCT_LINE_LOOKUP"."PRODUCT_LINE_EN" = '`. So, if the user enters the value as 'XYZ', the macro is replaced by the following filter:

```
and "SLS_PRODUCT_LINE_LOOKUP"."PRODUCT_LINE_EN" = 'XYZ'
```

Interestingly, if the user doesn't provide any prompt value, then the fourth argument is simply ignored. The macro is then replaced by the third argument which is in our case is `'and 1=1'`.

Hence, the second list returns all the rows when user doesn't provide any value for the prompt. This way it makes the `PRODUCT_LINE_EN` filter purely optional.

There's more...

Prompt macro accepts two more arguments (fifth and sixth). Please check the help documents or internet sources to find information and examples about them.

Adding token using macro

In this recipe, we will see how to dynamically change the field on which filter is being applied using macro. We will use prompt macro to generate one of the possible tokens and then use it in the query.

Getting ready

Create a list report based on native SQL similar to the previous recipe. We will use the same query that works on the product tables but filtering will be different. For that, define the SQL as following:

```
select distinct "SLS_PRODUCT_LINE_LOOKUP"."PRODUCT_LINE_EN" "Product_
line" , "SLS_PRODUCT_LOOKUP"."PRODUCT_NAME" "Product_name" , "SLS_
PRODUCT_COLOR_LOOKUP"."PRODUCT_COLOR_EN" "Product_color" , "SLS_
PRODUCT_SIZE_LOOKUP"."PRODUCT_SIZE_EN" "Product_size"
 from "GOSALESDW"."SLS_PRODUCT_DIM" "SLS_PRODUCT_DIM",
"GOSALESDW"."SLS_PRODUCT_LINE_LOOKUP" "SLS_PRODUCT_LINE_LOOKUP",
"GOSALESDW"."SLS_PRODUCT_TYPE_LOOKUP" "SLS_PRODUCT_TYPE_
LOOKUP", "GOSALESDW"."SLS_PRODUCT_LOOKUP" "SLS_PRODUCT_LOOKUP",
"GOSALESDW"."SLS_PRODUCT_COLOR_LOOKUP" "SLS_PRODUCT_COLOR_LOOKUP",
"GOSALESDW"."SLS_PRODUCT_SIZE_LOOKUP" "SLS_PRODUCT_SIZE_LOOKUP",
"GOSALESDW"."SLS_PRODUCT_BRAND_LOOKUP" "SLS_PRODUCT_BRAND_LOOKUP"
 where "SLS_PRODUCT_LOOKUP"."PRODUCT_LANGUAGE" = N'EN' and "SLS_
PRODUCT_DIM"."PRODUCT_LINE_CODE" = "SLS_PRODUCT_LINE_LOOKUP"."PRODUCT_
LINE_CODE" and "SLS_PRODUCT_DIM"."PRODUCT_NUMBER" = "SLS_PRODUCT_
LOOKUP"."PRODUCT_NUMBER" and "SLS_PRODUCT_DIM"."PRODUCT_SIZE_CODE"
= "SLS_PRODUCT_SIZE_LOOKUP"."PRODUCT_SIZE_CODE" and "SLS_PRODUCT_
DIM"."PRODUCT_TYPE_CODE" = "SLS_PRODUCT_TYPE_LOOKUP"."PRODUCT_TYPE_
```

```
CODE" and "SLS_PRODUCT_DIM"."PRODUCT_COLOR_CODE" = "SLS_PRODUCT_COLOR_
LOOKUP"."PRODUCT_COLOR_CODE" and "SLS_PRODUCT_BRAND_LOOKUP"."PRODUCT_
BRAND_CODE" = "SLS_PRODUCT_DIM"."PRODUCT_BRAND_CODE"
and
#prompt ('Field','token','"SLS_PRODUCT_LINE_LOOKUP"."PRODUCT_LINE_
EN"')# like #prompt ('Value','string')#
```

This is the same basic query that joins the product related tables and fetches required columns. The last statement in WHERE clause uses two prompt macros. We will talk about it in detail.

How to do it...

1. We have already created a list report based on an SQL query subject as mentioned previously. Drag the columns from the query subject on the list over the report page.

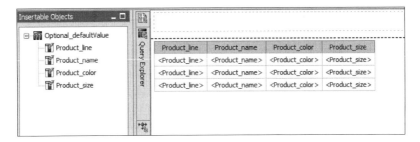

2. Now create a new prompt page.

3. Add a value prompt on the prompt page. Define two static choices for this.

Display value	Use value
Filter on product line	"SLS_PRODUCT_LINE_LOOKUP"."PRODUCT_LINE_EN"
Filter on product name	"SLS_PRODUCT_LOOKUP"."PRODUCT_NAME

4. Set the parameter for this prompt to 'Field'. This will come pre-populated as existing parameter, as it is defined in the query subject.

5. Choose the UI as radio button group and **Filter on Product Line** as default selection.

6. Now add a text box prompt on to the prompt page.

7. Set its parameter to **Value** which comes as a choice in an existing parameter (as it is already defined in the query).

8. Run the report to test it. You will see an option to filter on product line or product name. The value you provide in the text box prompt will be used to filter either of the fields depending on the choice selected in radio buttons.

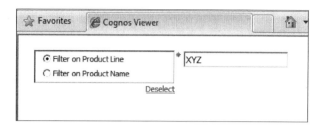

How it works...

The data type (second argument) of Prompt () function determines how the value is returned. For string type, the value is returned within a single quote. However, there is a data type called 'Token'. When you use this, function accepts a string value and puts it literally within the expression, that is, without quotes.

Here we have used this functionality to dynamically change the field on which filter is applied. The two possible tokens are defined in the USE VALUE of the radio button. Depending on the user's choice, one of the token will be placed in the query and will form the left part of filter expression.

Right part of the filter is a standard string parameter. Whatever value the user types in the text box prompt will be wrapped in single quotes and then placed in the SQL statement.

Effectively, the resulting expression will be something like this:

```
"SLS_PRODUCT_LINE_LOOKUP"."PRODUCT_LINE_EN" = 'XYZ'
```

Using prompt and promptmany macros in query subject

This recipe will show you that macros can be used with standard query subjects as well.

Getting ready

Create a simple list report based on **GO Sales Data Warehouse (Query)** package. Insert Product line, Product name, Product color, and Product size as the columns.

How to do it...

1. Go to **Query Explorer** and open the query used by list.

2. Add a detail filter with following definition:

   ```
   [Product line] = #prompt('ProductLine')#
   ```

3. Add another detail filter as follows:

   ```
   [Product name] in #promptmany('Product')#
   ```

4. Run the report to test it. You will see two mandatory prompts. The one for Product line will let you enter one value. Whereas the other one will be on product and it will allow you to enter multiple values.

How it works...

This is the same `Prompt()` macro which we used in prior recipes with native SQLs. As you can see, macros can be used in standard query subjects. You can utilize them in filters, data items, and slicers.

The strength of this feature is seen when you use the other macros like substitute, `CSVIdentityNameList`, `TimeStampMask`, and so on in data item and slicer.

Showing the prompt values in report based on security

This recipe combines the techniques learned in prior recipes to achieve a business requirement. A report shows sales data by country and product line. Users can choose to see data for one or more countries.

However, we need to implement a security mechanism such that a user can choose only those countries to which he is supposed to have access. This is determined by the user groups he belongs to.

Getting ready

Create a simple list report with **Country**, **City**, **Product line**, and **Sales Quantity** as columns.

How to do it...

1. We will start by adding a filter for countries. For that, go to **Query Explorer** and insert a new detail filter. Define it as: [Country] in ?Countries?

   Ensure that this filter is mandatory.

2. Now, add a new prompt page. Drag a value prompt on to it.

3. Follow the prompt wizard to set the following:

   a. Link it to existing parameter called 'Countries'.

   b. Create a new query for this prompt and call it 'Countries'.

4. Go to **Query Explorer** and open the **Countries** query subject.

5. Add a detail filter and define it as: [Country] in (#CSVIdentityNameList(',')#)

6. Run the report to test it. You will see that you can see only those countries in the value prompt to which the user is supposed to have access. For my account, I can see only 'Spain' as I have set the membership accordingly.

How it works...

This recipe simply combines the technique we learnt in prior recipes. We use CSVIdentityNameList() macro to retrieve the user group information.

We use this macro in the prompt query in order to restrict the values coming through in the value prompt. Whatever values are selected by users are then passed as a standard parameter for filtering to the report query.

String operations to get it right

We have seen one example of doing string manipulation in a macro to swap the columns of slicer in *Working with Dimensional Model* chapter. In this recipe, I will show you more macro functions to manipulate the values and achieve the required functionality using them.

A report is required to show sales by date and product lines. This report should show data only for current month (full month).

Getting ready

Create a simple list report with **Date**, **Product line**, and sales **Quantity** as columns.

Date	Product line	Quantity
<Date>	<Product line>	<Quantity>
<Date>	<Product line>	<Quantity>
<Date>	<Product line>	<Quantity>

How to do it...

1. Open **Query Explorer**. Go to the query used by the list object.

2. Add a new detail filter and define it as: `[Date] between #timestampMask (_first_of_month($current_timestamp),'yyyy-mm-dd')#` and `#timestampMask(_last_of_month($current_timestamp), 'yyyy-mm-dd')#`

3. Run the report to test it. Unfortunately, the GO Sales database doesn't hold data for year 2010. However, if you insert rows for current month in the database, you will see that they are retrieved by the report.

How it works...

Here I am introducing you to four new elements usable in macros. First one is a session parameter called `current_timestamp`. Session parameters are accessed in macro by putting a dollar sign ($) before them. `$current_timestamp` returns the current date and time on the Cognos server.

Then we use functions called `_first_of_month()` and `_last_of_month()`. These functions accept the date-time value and return corresponding first and last days of the month. For example, if today's date is 21st Jan 2010, then `#_first_of_month($current_timestamp)#` will return 1st Jan 2010.

Finally, we use the `timestampMask()` function to mask the time part and return date in required format. This function takes several format strings as second argument and we are passing `yyyy-mm-dd` for that.

This way we are using macros to determine the date range for current full month. We use them to filter the data in our detail filter.

You can use this concept to build up your own logic using different macro functions to achieve required functionalities, that are not available as standard in Cognos Report Studio.

There's more...

I would highly recommend checking out the other macro functions using Framework Manager.

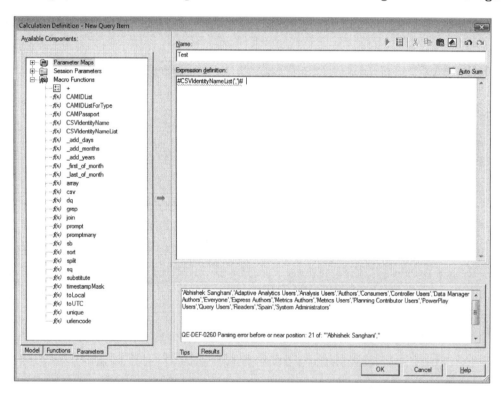

FM gives you a ready list of available functions, their descriptions, and a place to quickly try and test them.

Showing user name in footer

Let's examine two more session parameters which are very useful in real-life reports. Reports are often printed and handed over to other members/teams to have a look. For a person who is looking at a printed report, the most important thing is to know the time when the report was run. That is why we usually put the timestamp in the report footer.

However, it is useful to record who ran the report. This helps us to go back to the person in case of any queries. This recipe shows you how to display the user's name and the machine on which report was run in the footer.

Getting ready

Pick up any of the existing reports.

How to do it...

1. Go to **Query Explorer** and create a new query subject called **User**.

2. In that query subject, add a new data item. Call it **Machine** and define it as:
   `#sq($machine)#`

3. Then add another data item and call it as **User**. Define it as: `#sq($account.`
   `defaultName)#`

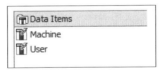

4. Now go to the report page. Select anything on the page. Using ancestor button, select the whole **Page** object.

5. For this, amend the **Query** property and link the page to **User** query subject.

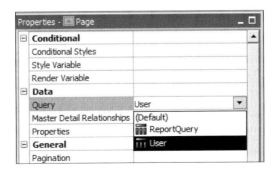

6. Now drag the **User** and **Machine** data items from 'Insertable objects' pane on the report footer.

7. Run the report to test it.

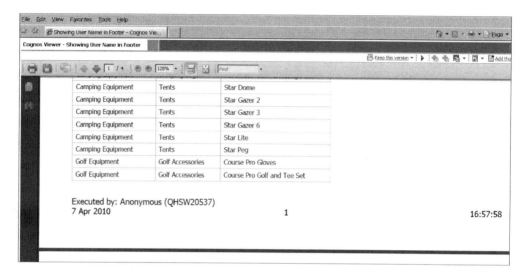

How it works...

Here we are using two session parameters, namely **$account.defaultName** and **$machine**. They are accessible within macro and a macro has to be written within a query subject. Hence, we create a new query subject to define these two items. Then we link the page with it and drag the items on the report footer.

The session parameter **$machine** has been introduced recently in Cognos Report Studio. It was made available from version 8.3 onwards.

There's more...

If the user directory is properly set up, you might be able to access more user information, such as email id, given names and surname.

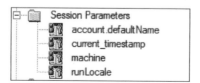

Please take your time to examine other session parameters using Framework Manager.

9
Using Report Studio Better

In this chapter, we will cover the following:

- ▶ Report Studio environmental options
- ▶ Copy-pasting partial or full reports
- ▶ Copy-pasting whole reports—8.2 to 8.4 possible
- ▶ Setting the execution time out
- ▶ Setting the maximum rows limit
- ▶ Handling slow report validation
- ▶ Capturing a query
- ▶ Browsing values from the data expression window
- ▶ The page structure view
- ▶ How to pick up and apply styles
- ▶ Grab them all practice

Introduction

It is a common issue in learning any rich tool that we tend to miss out some options or features that are not frequently used. We do routine development work without even knowing that there are some features that can improve our experience as a developer (report writer) or improve the deliverables.

This chapter will show you different customizable options and utilities within Cognos Report Studio that can make a report builder's life easier. They will save your time and effort and some will reduce the number of defects as well.

Though I have made some recommendations throughout these recipes depending on my personal preference, I suggest that you try these options yourself and then decide. Please refer to the Cognos manual for detailed information about each option and utility.

Report Studio environmental options

In this recipe, you will read about some environmental options that you can set in Report Studio to aid the development.

Getting ready

Create a simple list report with **Product line** and **Product name** as columns from **Product** query subject.

How to do it...

1. Select the **Product name** column. Using the **Ancestor** button in the **Properties** pane, select the **List Column** object.

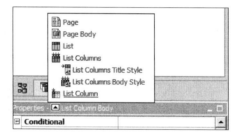

2. From the **Properties** pane, change the **Box Type** to **None**.

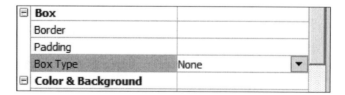

3. You will notice that you cannot see the **Product name** column on report page anymore. Now, assume that you want to change the **Box Type** back to **default**. It is difficult to do it as you cannot select the column now.

4. Now from the menu, select **View | Visual Aids | Show Hidden Objects**. You will notice that the **Product name** column becomes visible.

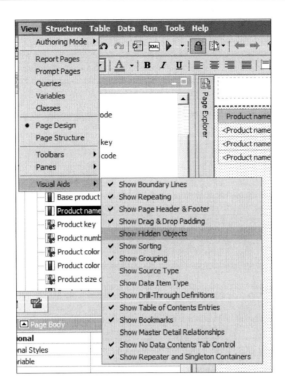

5. You can now select this column and change its properties as required.

6. Similarly, you can experiment with other options in **Visual Aid**.

7. Now we will see a crosstab-related feature.

8. Create a new crosstab on the report with **Product name** and **Product color** nested on rows.

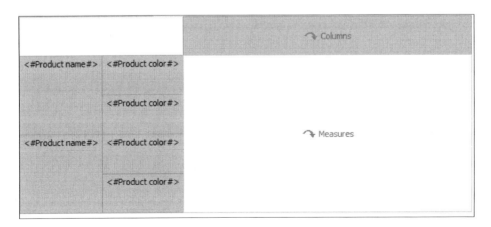

9. Now try to drag **Product size** beneath **Product name**. You will see that it will create a new node, without nesting **Product color** in it.

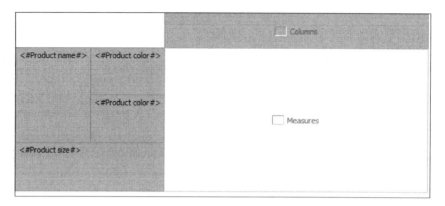

10. Now undo last operation and from the menu, select **Structure | Create Crosstab Nodes**. Uncheck this option.

11. Try to drag **Product size** again beneath **Product name**. You will notice that you can now insert it without creating a new crosstab node. It can be a peer of **Product name**, with **Product color** already nested in.

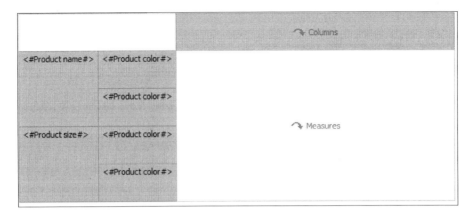

12. We will discuss about its usage in the "How it works" section.

13. Now, let us examine some options from the **Tools | Options** menu.

14. This dialog box has four tabs. The first tab is related to the look and feel of Report Studio. One important setting here is **Reuse Cognos Viewer window**.

15. Toggle this option and run the report multiples times. You will notice that when this option is turned off, Report Studio creates a new window for every execution of the report.

16. Take your time to examine the options from other tabs as well. The **Report** tab has some useful options which are discussed in the "How it works" section.

How it works...

Now let us talk in detail about the options we visited in this recipe.

View | Visual Aid

As the name suggests, these are some visual aids to help the report writer during development of report.

The option we experimented with toggled the visibility of hidden objects. Once an object is hidden, if it is not visible on report page, the only way to manipulate it is to go to **Page Structure**. We will talk about it in another recipe in this chapter. However, I personally prefer to "Show Hidden Objects" as it is very handy to select them from report page and manipulate.

Show Repeating is particularly useful when you have multiple levels of nesting and different Group Spans.

You should take your time to experiment with these options to decide on the ones you would like to keep.

Structure | Crosstab Node Creation Option

As we have already seen, when this option is on and a new item added to a crosstab, it is created as a crosstab node. Whereas, when this option is off, the new item is added to the existing node and retains the existing nesting.

It is advisable to turn this option off. This will allow you to create discontinuous crosstabs. Also, you can anyways manually add the same nesting as peer nodes, if you need to do so.

Tools | Options | View | Reuse Cognos Viewer Window

I prefer to turn this option off during development. By doing this, I can compare the report output with that of previous execution and see the effect of whatever changes I did. However, you might end up having loads of report viewer windows. So you should remember to close the ones which are not needed. Again, it is your personal choice to keep or reject this option.

Tools | Options | Report Options

Let us examine some useful options from this tab.

Option	Description
Alias member unique names	This is useful when working with dimensional models. If turned on, Report Studio creates a separate data item (alias) for any member dragged in expression.
	I prefer to keep this option off, as it unnecessarily increases the number of data items in query subject.

Option	Description
Delete unreferenced query objects	When on, Report Studio automatically deletes the query objects linked to another object that is deleted. For example, if you delete a list, the query subject linked to the list is deleted as well. I like this one as it helps in housekeeping.
	If you want to remove an object from one place but still keep it in other places, you can 'cut' it instead of 'delete' it.
Delete unreferenced conditional styles	Automatically deletes conditional styles when the last data item that refers to the conditional style is also deleted. This option is newly added in the latest versions.
Aggregation mode	This is a very useful option (recently added in newer versions) when working with a dimensional data source. It specifies the aggregation type to use when aggregating values in crosstabs and charts.
	Within detail aggregates the lowest level of visible details.
	Within aggregate aggregates the visible aggregates at the next lower level of detail.
	Within set aggregates the member sets. It considers members within current content and is faster than *Within Detail*.
	This can not only affect the result of the aggregation, but also the performance of report.

There's more...

You should refer to the Cognos Documentation to learn more about these options and then experiment with them to decide which are meant for you.

Copy-pasting partial or full report

Perhaps this is not something that is going to impress you. But I was really impressed when I saw this feature. We will see how to copy a part of report and full report and paste it into another instance.

We often need to copy a part of report or full report from one Report Studio environment or instance, to another. This might be for re-use purpose or for promoting it to the next stage.

Getting ready

We will use the report created in previous recipe for this one.

How to do it...

1. Open the report in Report Studio. We will call it the **Source** instance.

2. Now open another instance of Report Studio from same connection portal for same package [GO Data Warehouse (Query)]. We will call this instance **Destination**.

3. Now go to **Query Explorer** in both the instances.

4. Right click on **Query1** from the **Source** instance and choose **Copy**.

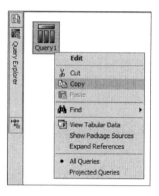

In the Query Explorer of the **Destination** instance, *right-click* and choose to *Paste*.

5. You will see that the Query Subject is successfully copied. You can open it and check the data items. They carry all the properties properly.

6. Now go to **Report Page** in the **Source** instance. Select the list object. This time hit *Ctrl+C* on the keyboard to copy it.

7. Switch to the **Destination** instance. Go to **Report Page**. Select the page body and hit *Ctrl+V* to paste the list object. Change the **Query** property of this list to **Query1**.

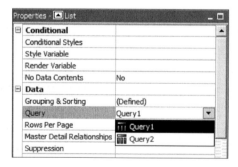

8. Run the report to test it. You will see that the list report is produced correctly.

9. Finally, we will see how to copy the whole report. For that, go back to the **Source** instance.

10. From the menu, choose **Tools | Copy Report to Clipboard**.

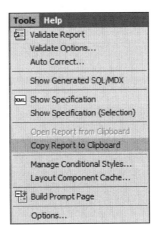

11. In the destination instance, from menu, choose **Tools | Open Report from Clipboard**.

12. You will see that the whole report has been copied to the destination instance. Here it is a new report that you can validate and save at an appropriate location.

How it works...

When a part of report is selected and copied (using *right click+Copy* or *Ctrl+C*), its XML specification is copied on the clipboard. You can paste it in any XML or Text Editor and examine. At destination instance, you can paste this XML specification and Report Studio properly parses it to create the objects.

When the copied object has some dependency, for example, list is dependant on the Query Subject then dependency object should be copied first. That is why we first copied the Query Subject, and then the list.

This feature is useful as it allows a quick re-use of objects and saves time.

The **Copy Report to Clipboard** and **Open Report from Clipboard** options are particularly useful in copying the reports across environments or servers. This comes in handy when the packages are promoted to destination environment and hence this saves the export-import hassles.

Copy-pasting whole reports—8.2 to 8.4 possible

This recipe will examine if we can use the copy-paste feature of Report Studio to promote a report from an older version to a newer version.

Getting ready

My dear readers might not be able to experiment with this. I will perform this recipe using two Cognos environments—8.2 and 8.4. Both the environments are configured and have GO Data Warehouse (Query) package published.

How to do it...

1. Open any report in Report Studio version 8.2.

2. From the menu, choose **Tools | Copy Report to Clipboard**.

3. Open Report Studio instance from higher version of Cognos. I will open one from 8.4. Choose GO Data Warehouse (Query) package.

4. In this new instance, select **Tools | Open Report from Clipboard** from the menu.

5. You will see the following dialog box:

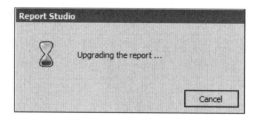

6. Run the report to test it. In most cases, the report will run fine.

How it works...

The newer versions of Cognos Report Studio are made backwards compatible when it comes to the XML specification of the report. That means we can copy the specification from an older version and paste it into a newer one. It will automatically detect the difference and will upgrade the specification accordingly.

Setting execution time out

Some reports are capable of firing quite resource consuming queries on the data source. This can cause a bottleneck on the database and hence a problem for other users and jobs. This recipe will show you how to automatically get the report query killed if it takes longer than a certain time limit.

Getting ready

Create a simple list report based on GO Data Warehouse (Query) package. Pull Product line, Product type, and Product name as columns.

How to do it...

1. Open the report in Cognos Report Studio.
2. Go to **Query Explorer** and select **Query1**.
3. From **Properties** pane, open **Maximum Execution Time** property.
4. Set it to a low number. For testing, we will set it to 1.

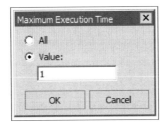

That means we are setting the maximum execution time for the query to one second.

5. Run the report to test it. In most cases, this will cross the threshold of one second and you will receive an error message like the one shown as follows:

RQP-DEF-0112

 Query execution time exceeds the 1 second limit specified for the user who has the identity '{Spain, Everyone, Authors, Query Users, Consumers, Metrics Authors, Metrics Users, Planning Contributor Users, Controller Users, Analysis Users, PowerPlay Users, Data Manager Authors, Readers, Express Authors, Adaptive Analytics Users, System Administrators}'.

6. Now go back to Cognos Report Studio and increase the **Maximum Execution Time** for query to **30 sec** and run the report. It will run fine.

How it works...

In this recipe, we experimented with the **Maximum Execution Time** property of the query. As you can see, this property allows us to terminate the report execution automatically if the query is taking a long time.

It is a useful property for reports where users can accidentally or purposely put some highly resource consuming selection parameters. For example, if a report is supposed to be run for a small date range, some users might mistakenly run it for months or years, hence hammering the database. This can take up a lot of database time and might also affect other jobs running on the server.

By putting a time limit on it, we can ensure that report is automatically terminated if it is going on for a certain length of time.

However, this time limit is not for the total time taken by the query on database. It is for the time lapsed from query submission to the first result returned back. In HTML output, often a page full of data is returned quickly and hence the report might not show an error. Whereas, when same report is run in PDF or Excel, it might reach the threshold and error.

Also, there is no easy way to customize the error message. As you can see, it is an ugly message, but we have to live with it.

There's more...

The maximum time limit can also be set at package level in Framework Manager using the **Governors**. Please refer to Framework Manager Documentation for the same.

The administrator can also define an environment-wide query execution time limit from **Connection Portal** by configuring the report service. For that, please refer to the *Administration and Security Guide*.

Setting maximum rows limit

This is similar to the previous recipe. Instead of setting any limit for query execution time, here we will set a restriction on the number of rows returned by the query.

Getting ready

We will use the report created in the previous recipe for this.

How to do it...

1. Open the report in Report Studio.
2. Go to **Query Explorer** and select the report query.
3. From the **Properties** pane, open **Maximum Rows Retrieved** property.
4. For testing purposes, set it to **50**.

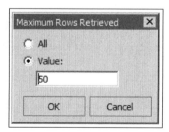

5. Run the report in HTML format.

6. Browse the report page by page. As soon as you hit the record count of 50 (usually on third page), you will receive an error message saying that the query has reached the maximum row limit.

RQP-DEF-0110

 The number of rows retrieved for the user who has the identity '{Spain, Everyone, Authors, Query Users, Consumers, Metrics Authors, Metrics Users, Planning Contributor Users, Controller Users, Analysis Users, PowerPlay Users, Data Manager Authors, Readers, Express Authors, Adaptive Analytics Users, System Administrators}' exceeds the limit of 50.

---

7. Go back to Cognos Report Studio and change the limit to required row limit. For example, 2000.

How it works...

This option serves same requirement as last recipe. When you want to ensure that the data source is not burdened by heavy queries, you should set such limits.

The maximum rows limit can also be set at package level from Framework Manager.

Handle slow report validation

Sometimes when you try to validate the report in Cognos Report Studio, it takes a long time. You will see 'validating' alert and then a blank dialog box appears and studio will seem to have frozen.

This recipe will show you how to fix this problem.

Getting ready

Create a simple report with all columns from **GO Data Warehouse (Query) | Sales | Product Query Subject.**

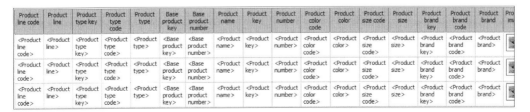

How to do it...

1. We will start by replicating the scenario that I am talking about. For that, open the **Query Explorer**.

2. Open the query associated with the list object. It is called **Query1** in the sample.

3. Add a detail filter with following definition:

   ```
   [Product line code] in ?PL?
   And [Product type] in ?Type?
   and [Product name] in ?Name?
   and [Product color] in ?Color?
   and [Product size] in ?Size?
   and [Product brand] in ?Brand?
   ```

4. Go back to report page. Now hit the **Validate** button from toolbar.

5. Notice that you first get the **Validating** alert. Then a new dialog box appears which is blank for a while.

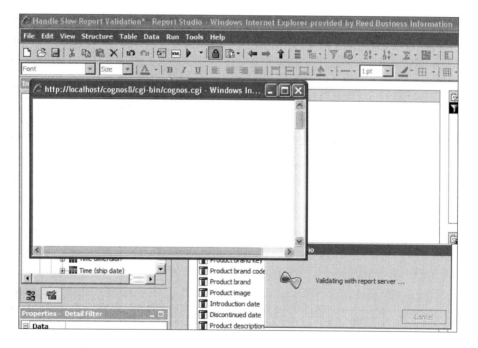

   Finally, all the prompts are loaded in that dialog box. You need to select each of them as all are mandatory. After making the selection, report validates.

6. Now go back to the **Query Subject**. Disable the **detail filter**.

7. Try validating the report now. You will see that validation is very quick now. You are not prompted for any selection and also the time to bring the prompts up is saved.

How it works...

When we validate any report in Cognos Report Studio, it asks us to enter the values for all the mandatory filters. This is a good thing as it forms the query with more completeness before validating. However, the prompt query and type of prompt are not controlled, which can often result in a long time to generate the prompt. This is annoying for the report writer as he/she only wants to do a sanity check on the report code.

By disabling the filter, we exclude it from the validation process. The Studio still validates everything else that is, data items, slicers, calculations, other query subjects, and so on.

This way we can stop the Cognos Report Studio from freezing or taking a long time for validating the report; still have a peace of mind that most of the report is validated. After validation is done, you should enable the filter again and then do test runs to ensure that the filters are working fine. You would do that anyways for Unit Testing.

There's more...

You can specify certain options related to report validation from menu. Select **Tools | Validation Options**. Here you can decide what level of information you would like to receive during the validation process. By default, it is set to **Warning**.

I recommend setting it to the most detailed, that is, **Information** level. This can provide some interesting and useful information about key transformation and query planning.

You can also decide whether you would like the query optimization to happen or not, by the **Interactive Data** option. When this is selected, the optimization is done and plan is created to retrieve the top rows depending on the "Execution Optimization" property of the query subject. By default, this option is unchecked. That means query is planned for retrieval of All Rows. I recommend keeping it to the default that is, unchecked.

Capturing query

Report Studio is a tool for wider audience—right from business users, management personnel and analysts, to the pure technical report writers. If you are a technical person who understands the SQL/MDX being fired on the database, you certainly want to examine one to optimize the report performance and sometimes to merely ensure that everything is fine.

This recipe will talk about the right ways to capture the query fired on data source.

Getting ready

We will use the list report created in the previous recipe for this.

How to do it...

1. Open the report in Cognos Report Studio.

2. Go to **Query Explorer** and set the **Usage** of the filter item to **Optional**.

3. From the menu, select **Tools | Show Generated SQL/MDX**.

4. A new dialog box will appear with the SQL statements for each query subject. (only **Query1** in this example)

5. Choose **Native SQL** from the dropdown. Examine the SQL statement.

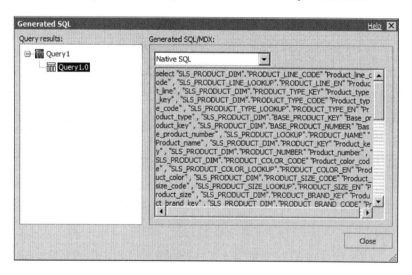

6. You will notice that there are no filters in the WHERE condition.

7. Now, close this dialog box. Change the **Usage** of filter to **Mandatory**.

8. Again, choose **Tools | Show Generated SQL/MDX** from the menu. You will be asked to enter prompt values. Enter some and click **OK**.

9. Check the Native SQL. This time you will see that filters are included in the `WHERE` clause.

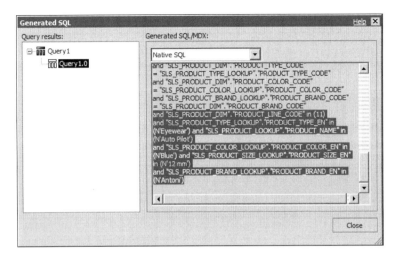

This is a query with more completeness which gives a better idea of what statement will be executed on the database when users run the report.

How it works...

The Generated SQL/MDX option gives you two types of queries: **Cognos SQL** and **Native SQL**. **Cognos SQL** is a generic and more readable form which also uses some Cognos function. However, it is not exact query that is fired on the database. For that, we need to refer to **Native SQL**.

Why make filters mandatory?

In the last recipe, I recommended that you disable the filters before validating. That was to exclude the query and speed up the validation. However, we have a different requirement here. Our report writing is almost done, and all data items, calculations, filters, slicers, and so on are defined. We now want to examine the actual query that will be fired on database, to examine the correctness of joins and filtering, and check any optimization possibilities.

For that purpose, we need the completeness of query. Hence, I am now asking you to change all the filters to **Mandatory**. That way, we force Cognos Report Studio to prompt you for the values and then include all the filters in the query.

Query formatting

The Native Query in this dialog box is not formatted and hence is very difficult to read. I recommend using some query formatting tools for that.

Many database clients and utilities like TOAD can be used to format SQL statements. You can also use online tools like http://www.dpriver.com/pp/sqlformat.htm.

If you are writing the report against dimensional source, the query will be of MDX type. http://mdx.mosha.com/ can be useful for formatting it.

Capture the query for database

It is recommended that you use the tracing utilities to directly trap the query from server. That way you can examine the timing and behavior. When you run the report in HTML format, Cognos might be asking for just a set of data. When you use **Sections** in the report, there will be multiple queries fired on database for a loop of values. All this can be studied only by directly examining the activities on database server. The Session Browser in TOAD and Profiler for SQL Server are classic examples of such utilities.

Browsing values from data expression window

This recipe will show you a small feature of Cognos Report Studio that comes very handy and is often overlooked.

Getting ready

We will use the report used in previous recipes for this.

How to do it...

1. Open the report in Report Studio.
2. Say we want this report to show only certain Product lines (hard-coding). For that we want to add a filter on Product Lines. So, add a new detail filter.
3. Now, we are in the filter expression dialog. Enter following expression:
   ```
   [Product Line] in
   ```

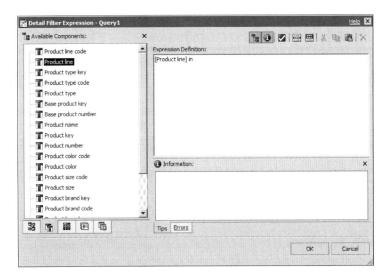

4. As this filter will do literal string comparisons, we need to enter the exact values of the required Product lines. Select the **Product line** data item from the **Data Items** pane. Hit the **Select Multiple Values** button 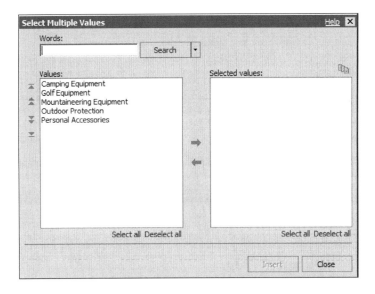 in the upper right of the page (located beside the **CUT** icon).

5. This will open a new dialog box.

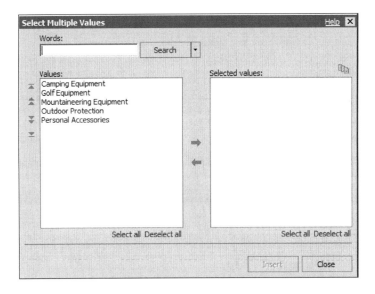

Select **Camping Equipment** and **Golf Equipment**. Hit the green arrow to add them to the list on right. Finally, close this dialog by clicking the **Insert** button.

6. You will see that the selected values are automatically populated in the filter expression and the expression now reads like this:

    ```
    [Product line] in ('Camping Equipment', 'Mountaineering
    Equipment')
    ```

7. Close the dialog box and run the report to test it.

How it works...

We often need to hard-code some data values in reports. This may be to restrict the data set, or to perform some conditional logic, or some other requirements. In order to define the values correctly, we need to browse the data and make sure that we write them correctly in the expression.

Instead of opening a database client to browse these values, this utility in Cognos Report Studio comes very handy. Sometimes, the report authors don't even have the database clients installed and configured on their machine.

You will see these two buttons in Cognos Report Studio when you are in the data item expression or filter expression dialog box.

Both will let you browse the values of the selected data item or query item. However, the first one will allow you to select only one value to be inserted in the expression. Whereas, the other one will allow you to select multiple values and will add them to the expression as comma delimited and within brackets.

There's more...

You can also test the data of the whole query subject (all query items, with the filters and slicers applied on result) by opening the Query Subject in Query Explorer; and choosing **Run | View Tabular Data** from the menu.

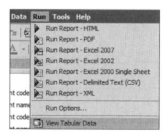

Please try this option to see how it works.

Page structure view

This recipe will show you another view/option available in Cognos Report Studio to examine and edit the reports.

Getting ready

We will use the same report used in the last recipe for this.

How to do it...

1. Open the report in Report Studio and go to the report page.

2. From the menu, choose **View | Page Structure**.

3. You will see the report page transforms into a tree-type list object.

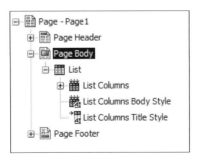

4. Open different nodes and examine the objects.

How it works...

As you know, the report definitions in Cognos Report Studio are nothing but XML files. The report objects, Page, List, Columns, and so on are all stored internally as nested tags.

By switching to **Page Structure** view, you can actually see how the objects are contained within each other and are inter-related. You can select any object (for example, List Columns Body Style) and manipulate its properties. You can also delete them, copy the objects and paste them in another place, and move them around within the rules governed by Cognos Report Studio.

This is a great way to examine and manipulate some report objects that are not directly visible in the normal view. We had mentioned in the 'Report Studio Environmental Options' recipe that when you hide some objects on the report page, and if the hidden items are not made visible by changing the environment options, then the only way to select and manipulate them is to do it from **Page Structure View**.

I would recommend that you familiarize yourself with this view. Do some browsing, copying / deleting of objects, and try changing properties of some objects. Later, you can go back to the normal view by selecting **View | Page Design** from the menu.

Pick-up and apply style

We will see a very useful utility within Cognos Report Studio newly introduced from version 8.3 onwards.

Getting ready

We will use the same list report that we used in the last recipe for this.

How to do it...

1. In this recipe, we will apply certain formatting to the list columns. Start by applying the following to the **Product line** column.

   Font: 12 pt

   Background Color: #FFFF99

   Border: 1pt solid lines on left and right. None for Top and Bottom.

2. Select the **Product line** column. Hit the **Pick-up Style button** ⟡ from toolbar.

3. Now select Product type, Product name, and Product number columns from the list (by holding *Ctrl* key).

4. Click the **Apply Style** button. ⟡

5. You will see that all the formatting, font, background color, and borders are applied to the selected columns.

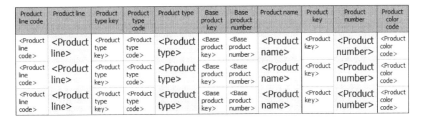

6. Now again select the **Product line** column.

7. This time click on the little dropdown (arrow) beside the **Pickup Style** button. Choose the **Edit Dropper Style** option.

8. This will open up a dialog box with the style already filled in. We don't want to copy the color for rest of the columns. We need only font and borders. So change the background color to **Default**.

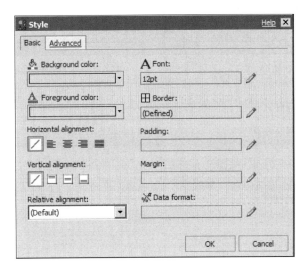

Click the **OK** button to close the dialog.

9. Now choose the rest of the columns from list (the ones which are not formatted). Hit the **Apply Style** button. Notice that the fonts and borders are applied to these columns and background color remains as default.

Product line code	Product line	Product type key	Product type code	Product type	Base product key	Base product number	Product name	Product key
<Product line code>	<Product line>	<Product type key>	<Product type code>	<Product type>	<Base product key>	<Base product number>	<Product name>	<Product key>
<Product line	<Product line>	<Product type	<Product type	<Product type>	<Base product	<Base product	<Product name>	<Product key>

10. Run the report to test it.

How it works...

Pick Up Style and **Apply Style** are buttons added to Cognos Report Studio from version 8.3 onwards. They work in conjunction and are extremely useful to the report writer.

As you have seen in the recipe, it allows the writer to pick-up or copy the styling of an object and then apply it to one or more objects in the report. You can choose to apply all the styles (colors, fonts, border, alignments, padding, formatting, data format, images, and so on) or just apply the selected ones.

From experience, it is seen that a lot of time is spent in formatting the reports that have large number of columns, rows, aggregations, and so on. Also, this is the area causing cosmetic defects in the reports. Using this utility, we can save quite some time and prevent defects too.

Grab them all practice

This recipe will tell you about something which is good practice. But I have put it under 'Using Report Studio Better' for two reasons. One—it builds upon the idea learnt in previous recipe. Two—it does help you use Report Studio better.

The last recipe showed you how to apply style to selected list columns. Here we will see the recommended way to apply same style to all the objects (List Column Titles in this case).

Getting ready

We will continue working on the report that we modified in the last recipe.

How to do it...

1. Say we want to apply the following style to all the list column titles.

   Font: 12 Pt

   Background Color: Silver

   Border: 1pt Solid all sides

   Then we have two options. First apply this style to one column title. Say **Product line code**.

Product line code	Product line	Product type key	Product type code	Product type	Base product key	
\<Product line code\>	\<Product line\>	\<Product type key\>	\<Product type code\>	\<Product type\>	\<Base product key\>	
\<Product	\<Product	\<Product	\<Product	\<Product	\<Base	

2. Now do the same **Pick-up Style** and **Apply Style** to all column titles as learnt in the previous recipe.

3. Run the report to test it and you will see that it works.

Product line code	Product line	Product type key	Product type code	Product type	Base product key	Base product number	Product name	Product key
2101	Camping Equipment	101	101	Cooking Gear	1	1	TrailChef Water Bag	30001

4. However, if you drag a few more columns on the list, you will see that the formatting needs to be re-done on them.

Discontinued date	Product description	Quantity	Unit cost	Unit price
\<Discontinued date\>	\<Product description\>	\<Quantity\>	\<Unit cost\>	\<Unit price\>

5. To avoid this problem, let's learn another technique. Remember that we want to apply the same formatting to all column titles. So, undo all the change we did to the report in this recipe. Bring it back to the original state as we left it in the last recipe.

6. Now select any one list column title.

7. Using the **Ancestor** button ▣ in **Property** pane, choose **List Column Title Style**. You will notice that all column titles are selected.

8. Now apply the required formatting (color, border, and font in this example).

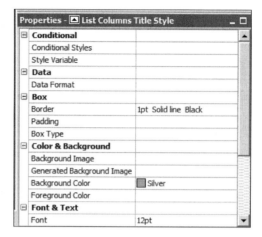

9. Run the report to test it.

10. Add some new columns to the list. Notice that the column titles already have consistent formatting.

Introduction date	Discontinued date	Product description	Quantity	Unit cost	Unit price
<Introduction date>	<Discontinued date>	<Product description>	<Quantity>	<Unit cost>	<Unit price>

How it works...

What we are doing here is, instead of selecting the column titles individually, making a general selection of 'List Column Title Style' that applies to all column titles. In fact it is a parent object, so even the new items added later on to the list will fall under it and will carry same formatting.

This practice of selecting a generic or parent-level object not only saves time but also makes the formatting more future-proof. A report writer should follow this 'grab it all' practice for the formatting that applies across.

There's more...

Please don't miss the 'Customizing Classes for report-wide effect' recipe in *Chapter 11, Best Practices*; to further enhance the technique of applying a universal style to the report.

10
Some More Useful Recipes

In this chapter, we will cover the following:

- ▶ Timing report execution
- ▶ Missing values versus spaces
- ▶ Overriding data formatting defined in database
- ▶ Setting up conditional drills
- ▶ Dynamically switching reports using an iFrame

Introduction

In this chapter, we will see some more useful tricks or techniques.

Timing report execution

We often want to record the exact time taken by a report to execute. This recipe will show you a technique that is tried and tested and can be used repeatedly to examine the performance of a report at different loads and volumes on the data source.

Getting ready

Take any report whose execution time is to be recorded. The steps for this recipe are to be carried out in Cognos Connection portal, not Cognos Report Studio.

How to do it...

1. Go to **Connection Portal** and locate the report.

2. Click on the **Create Report View** button ▦ and create a report view of this report in the desired location.

3. Open the **Properties** of the report view by clicking **Set Properties** button. ▤

4. Go to the **Report View** tab. Uncheck the **Prompt for values** option.

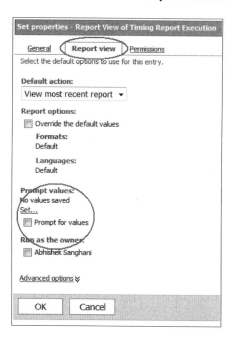

5. Click on the **Set** link for **Prompt values**. This will bring the prompt page up.

6. Select the prompt values and save them. Click the **OK** button to come back to the list of reports and report views.

7. Now click on the **Run with options** button ▷ and choose following options:

    a. Format: PDF

    b. Delivery: Save the report

    c. Uncheck the option of prompt for values

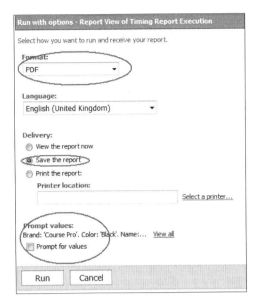

Click the **Run** button.

8. Now open the **Schedule Management** or **Past Activities** view. Once the report is executed, record the **Start time** and **Completion time**.

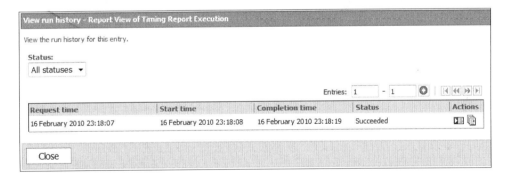

How it works...

Here we are creating a report view so that prompt values can be saved and then we run it in the background so that timing can be noted from schedule management.

Report view

Report view sits on top of the report. You can set different properties for it (delivery method, output format, and so on) as well as the prompt values; without affecting the actual report. If the main report is updated, the changes are automatically reflected in the view.

Scheduling

When we choose the delivery method as 'Save Report Output', the report execution happens in the background using the batch processing service. Using the schedule management view (or Past Activities view in version 8.4), we can see when exactly the report execution started and when it ended. This gives us the exact time taken by the report to execute.

When users use the report interactively, they tend to prefer output in HTML format. This retrieves only a pageful of data at a time, and hence the time taken to produce the first page does not accurately reflect the time that will be required to generate the whole report. Also, checking the time manually can be error prone. Hence it is advisable to use the scheduler as shown in the recipe, and do several runs with different prompt selections, to record the execution timings.

There's more...

You can create multiple report views of the same report to choose different prompt values and output formats.

Also, whenever you want to run performance tests on a particular data source, you can create a job to run all the report views against that data source. This will allow you to record the timings for all and compare them with prior runs.

Missing value versus zero value

Missing values in the data source can mean two things in real business—either the data is zero or it is missing. For example, in the case of a sales transaction based system, if there is no data for a product for a certain month, it means there was no sale of that product in that month. However, in some other system; for example, yearly returns of different stocks missing data might just mean that the data is not available for a certain reason. However, it certainly doesn't mean the return was zero.

Hence, it is important to clearly highlight the missing value as zero or missing in the report.

Getting ready

Create a simple crosstab report with all **Product line** on rows and **Month key** on columns from **GO Data Warehouse (Query) | Sales**. Choose sales quantity and unit cost as measures.

Quantity	<#Month key#>		<#Month key#>	
	<#Quantity#>	<#Unit cost#>	<#Quantity#>	<#Unit cost#>
<#Product line#>	<#1234#>	<#1234#>	<#1234#>	<#1234#>
<#Product line#>	<#1234#>	<#1234#>	<#1234#>	<#1234#>

How to do it...

1. First of all, we will run the report to see if there are any missing values.

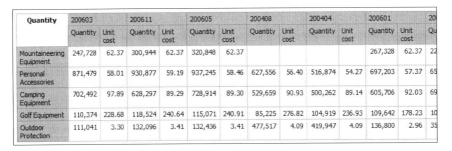

Quantity	200603		200611		200605		200408		200404		200601		20
	Quantity	Unit cost	Quantity	Unit cost	Quantity	Unit cost	Quantity	Unit cost	Quantity	Unit cost	Quantity	Unit cost	Qu
Mountaineering Equipment	247,728	62.37	300,944	62.37	320,848	62.37					267,328	62.37	22
Personal Accessories	871,479	58.01	930,877	59.19	937,245	58.46	627,556	56.40	516,874	54.27	697,203	57.37	65
Camping Equipment	702,492	97.89	628,297	89.29	728,914	89.30	529,659	90.93	500,262	89.14	605,706	92.03	69
Golf Equipment	110,374	228.68	118,524	240.64	115,071	240.91	85,225	276.82	104,919	236.93	109,642	178.23	10
Outdoor Protection	111,041	3.30	132,096	3.41	132,436	3.41	477,517	4.09	419,947	4.09	136,800	2.96	35

We can see that the **Sales Quantity** and **Unit Price** are missing for certain columns.

2. Now go to Report Studio and choose the **Quantity** measure from crosstab intersection.

3. From **Properties** pane, open the **Data Format** dialog. Set the **Format type** to **Number** and **Missing Value Characters** to **0**.

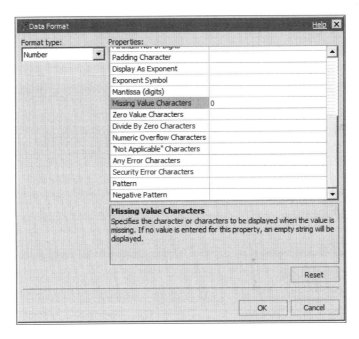

4. Similarly, set the data format for the unit price measure. However, this time set the **Missing Value Characters** to **N/A**.

5. Run the report to test it.

Quantity	200603		200611		200605		200408		200404		200601		200!
	Quantity	Unit cost	Quantity	Unit cost	Quantity	Unit cost	Quantity	Unit cost	Quantity	Unit cost	Quantity	Unit cost	Qua
Mountaineering Equipment	247,728	62.37	300,944	62.37	320,848	62.37	0	N/A	0	N/A	267,328	62.37	228
Personal Accessories	871,479	58.01	930,877	59.19	937,245	58.46	627,556	56.40	516,874	54.27	697,203	57.37	659
Camping Equipment	702,492	97.89	628,297	89.29	728,914	89.30	529,659	90.93	500,262	89.14	605,706	92.03	693
Golf Equipment	110,374	228.68	118,524	240.64	115,071	240.91	85,225	276.82	104,919	236.93	109,642	178.23	106
Outdoor Protection	111,041	3.30	132,096	3.41	132,436	3.41	477,517	4.09	419,947	4.09	136,800	2.96	359

How it works...

As discussed earlier, the missing values can mean different things. Here, when the sales quantity is missing, we know the sale was zero for the product for that period. However, the missing unit price doesn't mean it was zero. It just means that there is no data for that combination.

By setting appropriate **Missing Value Characters** we are ensuring that the correct message is conveyed through the report.

There's more...

You can also specify characters to be displayed in case of **Zero Values**, **Divide by Zero**, and some more conditions.

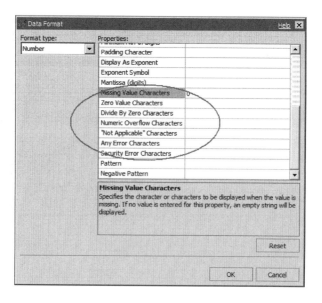

Over-riding data formatting defined in database

In Cognos Report Studio, we can define the formatting of data items that we have seen in many recipes. However, sometimes, the formatting defined in the report does not take effect. In this recipe, we will consider one such scenario.

Getting ready

We will use the dimensional **GO Sales SSAS Cube** package for this.

Open the **GOSALESDW** cube in the SQL Server **BIDS** (**Business Intelligence Development Studio**) and change the data format of the **Stmt Month** measure as shown in the following screenshot:

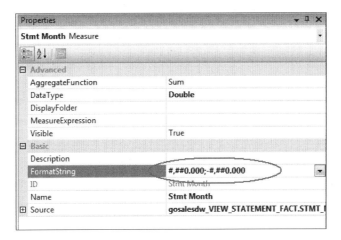

Process the cube. Create a new crosstab report in Cognos Report Studio against the **GO Sales SSAS Cube** package.

How to do it...

1. Drag **Organization Code1** on to rows, **Current Month** on to columns and **Stmt Month** as the measure.

2. Select the **Stmt Month** measure and define its data format to be **Number** and decimal points to **1**.

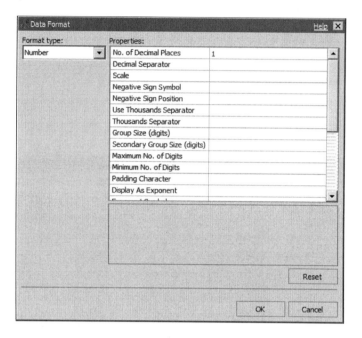

3. Run the report to test it. You will notice that the formatting is not reflected in the output.

Stmt Month	Opening balance Opening balance 2004	1 January 2004	2 February 2004	3 March 2004	4 April 2004	5 May 2004
Great Outdoors Consolidated Inc.	38,804,157,190.330	-103,024,047.680	231,634,118.460	628,077,220.080	976,754,402.310	1,349,074,290.410

4. Now, go back to Cognos Report Studio. Select the measure and open the data format again.

5. This time defines the pattern as shown in the following screenshot:

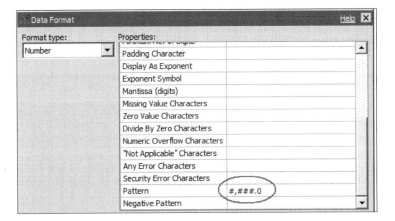

6. Run the report to test it. This time report will show numbers up to one decimal point only.

How it works...

As you saw in this recipe, from a glance it looks like the database formatting is taking precedence over the one defined in report studio. However, actually the formatting defined in the backend is a pattern. In order to correctly over-ride it, we need to define pattern in the report studio. Just over-riding the decimal points won't work.

Conditional drill-through

Cognos Report Studio allows you to define drill-through. However, there is no facility to define conditional drill-through. This recipe will show you how to achieve it.

We will use the report created in the previous recipe for this. We will create drill through from the crosstab intersection to a dummy report (drill 1). Then we will try to achieve a conditional drill-through to another report (drill 2) for certain months.

Getting ready

Create two dummy reports called **Drill 1** and **Drill 2**.

Open the report created in previous recipe in Cognos Report Studio.

How to do it...

1. First of all create drill-through from the crosstab intersection to the first report (Drill 1). We saw how to create such drill in earlier chapters of this book.

2. Now select the text item from crosstab intersection, hold *Ctrl* key on the keyboard and drag the text item a little to the left. This will create a copy of this text item within same intersection.

3. For this newly created copy of the text item, update the drill-through link to point to Drill 2.

4. Now we will define the condition to switch between the links. Create a Boolean variable called `Is_2004`. Define the condition as: `[Query1].[Current Month] contains '2004'`

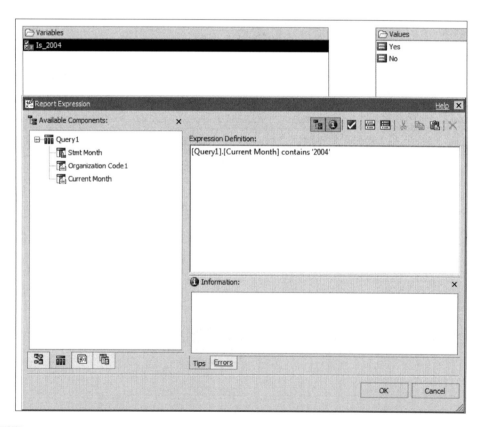

5. Go back to the report page. Attach the conditional variable `Is_2004` as **Style Variable** to both the drill links.

6. Using **Conditional Explorer**, set the **Box Type** to **None** for the left link when `Is_2004` is **Yes** and same for the right link when `Is_2004` is **No**.

   That is, turn the visibility off for one of the links, depending on the condition.

7. Run the report to test it.

How it works...

Within the drill-through definitions dialog box, there is no reference to the conditional variables. So, Report Studio provides no direct way to switch the drill target depending on a condition.

As a solution, we are creating a copy of the text item here and then we hide one of them based on a condition. As the text items go to different targets, we achieve conditional drill-through in the report.

There's more...

Instead of using the **Style Variable** and **Box Type**, we can use **Render Variable** to directly set when the item should be visible. However, in order to use **Render Variable**, we will need to use **String Variable** instead of **Boolean**.

Dynamically switching reports using iFrame

In this recipe, we will see how to use one report as a container to call or display different reports. We will use an HTML element called iFrame that allows the browser window to be split into segments. Each segment can be updated separately.

We will give users the ability to choose which report contents to display and toggle between two reports by clicking the appropriate button. You can build upon this idea to create many practical solutions like displaying help, toggling graphs, providing tabs to display different reports, and so on.

Getting ready

Create a simple list report with Product related columns (Product query subject) and save it as **iFrame–Products**.

Product line	Product type	Product name	Product color
<Product line>	<Product type>	<Product name>	<Product color>
<Product line>	<Product type>	<Product name>	<Product color>
<Product line>	<Product type>	<Product name>	<Product color>

Create another simple list report with Retailer related columns (Retailer query subject) and save this report as **iFrame–Retailers**.

Retailer type	Retailer name
<Retailer type>	<Retailer name>
<Retailer type>	<Retailer name>
<Retailer type>	<Retailer name>

How to do it...

1. Go to **Connection Portal** and locate the reports we created previously.

Click on the **Set Properties** button for 'iFrame –Products'. From **General** tab, click the **View search path** link.

Copy the **Default Action URL** and save it somewhere for use in later steps. This URL will look similar to: http://localhost:80/cognos8/cgi-bin/cognos.cgi?b_action=cognosViewer&ui.action=run&ui.object=%2fcontent%2fpackage%5b%40name%3d%27GO%20Data%20Warehouse%20(query)%27%5d%2ffolder%5b%40name%3d%27Chapter%2010%27%5d%2freport%5b%40name%3d%27iFrame%20-%20Products%27%5d&ui.name=iFrame%20-%20Products&run.outputFormat=&run.prompt=true

2. Similarly save the **Default Action URL** for 'iFrame – Retailers' report.

3. Now go to Cognos Report Studio and create a new blank report.

4. On the report page, drag a new **HTML Item** to the page. Define the code as follows:

```
<script language="javascript" type="text/javascript">
function showReport(x)
{
switch(x)
{
/* Replace the URL in below stmt with the one you saved for
iFrame-Product report */

case 1: document.getElementById("dynamic_report").src = "http://
localhost:80/cognos8/cgi-bin/cognos.cgi?b_action=cognosViewer&ui.
action=run&ui.object=%2fcontent%2fpackage%5b%40name%3d%27
GO%20Data%20Warehouse%20(query)%27%5d%2ffolder%5b%40name%
3d%27Chapter%2010%27%5d%2freport%5b%40name%3d%27iFrame%20
-%20Products%27%5d&ui.name=iFrame%20-%20Products&run.
outputFormat=&run.prompt=true&cv.toolbar=false&cv.header=false";
break;

/* Replace the URL in below stmt with the one you saved for
iFrame-Retailer report */

case 2: document.getElementById("dynamic_report").src = "http://
localhost:80/cognos8/cgi-bin/cognos.cgi?b_action=cognosViewer&ui.
action=run&ui.object=%2fcontent%2fpackage%5b%40name%3d%27
GO%20Data%20Warehouse%20(query)%27%5d%2ffolder%5b%40name%
3d%27Chapter%2010%27%5d%2freport%5b%40name%3d%27iFrame%20
-%20Retailers%27%5d&ui.name=iFrame%20-%20Retailers&run.
outputFormat=&run.prompt=true&cv.toolbar=false&cv.header=false";
break;
}
}
</script>
<button type="button" onclick="showReport(1);">Products</button>
<button type="button" onclick="showReport(2);">Retailers</button>
```

For the URL shown in bold, you need to place the Default Action URLs that you saved for both the reports in the first step.

5. Now create another **HTML item** on the report page and define the code as:

    ```
    <iframe name="dynamic_report" src="" frameborder="0" height="90%"
    width="100%"></iframe>
    ```

6. The report will look like a blank page with two HTML items on it.

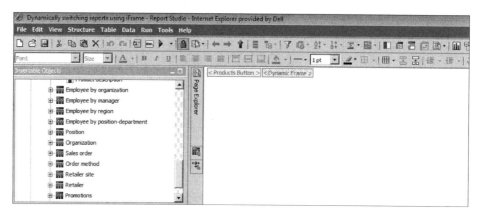

7. Run the report to test it. You should see two buttons called **Products** and **Retailers**. When you click on **Products**, the 'iFrame – Products' report will be displayed. By clicking on the **Retailers** button, you can display the 'iFrame – Retailers' report.

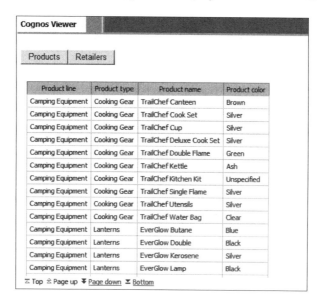

How it works...

Here we are using the **iFrame** element of HTML to achieve dynamic content on the report page. In one HTML item, we define an iFrame element called `dynamic_report` and set it's source (`src` property) to blank.

Then in another HTML item, we define two buttons and one JavaScript to dynamically change the source (`src`) property of the iFrame. Depending on which button is clicked, we set the source of iFrame to the Default Action URL of either 'iFrame-Product' report or 'iFrame-Retailers' report.

When the report first loads, the iFrame is empty (because the source property is blank). As soon as user clicks on any of the buttons, the iFrame source is changed by the JavaScript. This causes either of the reports to execute and the output is loaded on the page. This way it allows us to dynamically switch between the report contents while staying on the same page.

There's more...

Please note that you should append `&cv.toolbar=false&cv.header=false` to the URLs in the JavaScript. This would hide the Cognos toolbar and header from showing up again in the iFrame.

Also, you should try and extend this concept to create other dynamic solutions, for example like displaying help, toggling graphs, providing tabs to display different reports, and so on.

11
Best Practices

In this chapter, we will cover:

- ▶ Reducing the number of query items
- ▶ Highlighting hidden items
- ▶ Relative paths for images
- ▶ Taming JavaScripts
- ▶ Customizing classes to report-wide effect
- ▶ Creating templates
- ▶ Regression testing
- ▶ Code commenting

Introduction

In this chapter, we will see some best practices followed in the world of Cognos Report Development. Once you learn them and start using them in your day-to-day life, you will notice that these practices not only save your time but also reduce the number of defects and benefit the ongoing maintenance of reports.

Reducing number of query items

From the maintenance and documentation perspective, it is advisable to keep the number of query items in report query subjects to the minimal. In this recipe, we will see some good practices to ensure this.

Getting ready

We will use the dimensional **GO Sales SSAS Cube** package for this.

From **Tools | Options**, check the options of **Alias member unique name** and uncheck **Delete unreferenced query objects**.

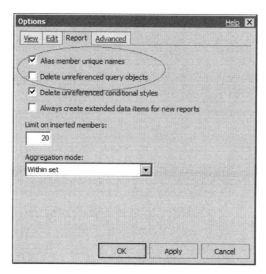

How to do it...

1. We will start by creating a simple crosstab report. Open Cognos Report Studio for a new crosstab report. **Drag Time Month Dim | Current Year level** on the columns.

2. From the **Insertable Objects** pane, drag a new **Set Expression** on rows.

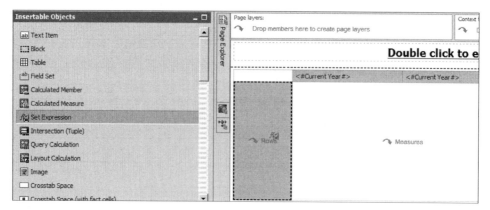

3. Give it a name, for example, **Accounts** and choose the **Account Dim** hierarchy.

4. In the **Data Item Expression** window, expand the **Account Dim** hierarchy to locate children of **Assets (total)**.

5. Select the three children of **Assets (total)** and drag them onto the expression definition. They will appear as comma separated values. Put them within a SET ( ) function.

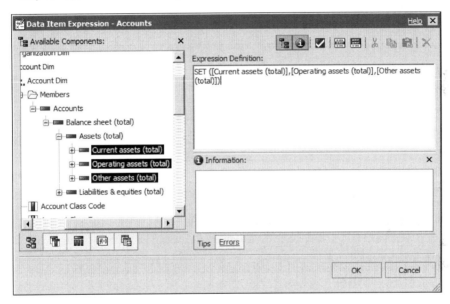

6. Pull **Stmt Year** from the measures in the crosstab intersection.

7. Run the report to test it. It should work fine. Now go back to the studio and examine the report **Query Subject**.

8. You will notice that there are six query items.

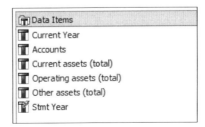

9. Now go back to Report Page and delete the **Current Year** from columns. Drag **Current Month** there instead.

10. Go back to Query Explorer to examine the query subject. Notice that both, **Current Year** and **Current Month** are present.

11. Run the report to test. It works fine. However, there is a redundant item in the query subject (that is, **Current Year**) which is not used anywhere in the report.

12. Now go back to Cognos Report Studio. From **Tools | Options**, uncheck the options of **Alias member unique name** and check **Delete unreferenced query objects** (opposite of what we had in the beginning).

13. Delete the crosstab from report page. Again create it by following steps 1 to 9. Examine the query subject this time. You will see that only three query items are present this time.

14. Finally, we will try one more thing. Select the **Current Month** from columns and hit *Ctrl+X* to cut it. You will see that it is removed from crosstab.

15. If we want to bring it back, we have two places. Either, we can drag it from the **Model/Source** pane, or we can get it from **Data Items** pane.

16. First drag it from the model or source tab. Notice it is called 'Current Month 1' now and a duplicate query item is created for it in the query subject.

17. Hit the **Undo** button. Drag it this time for the **Data Item** pane. Notice that no new data item is created this time.

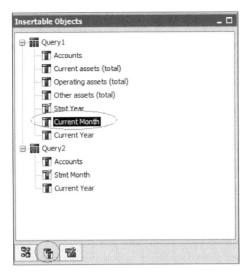

How it works...

We have already talked about the environment options in this book previously. This recipe highlights how these options can be useful in reducing the number of query items.

Alias member unique name

By checking this option, we make Cognos Report Studio create a new data item for each member used within any data item or filter. This means a greater number of query items. We uncheck this option to stop the creation of separate aliases.

Delete unreferenced query objects

When this is unchecked, the data items that you delete from the report page are still maintained within the query subject. Hence, we check this option to automatically clear the unused items. You can still 'Cut' the item from report purposely to keep it in the query subject, if required.

Dragging items from data items pane

Whenever an item is already present in query subject, if it needs to be pulled again on the corresponding container, it should be pulled from data items pane. Dragging it again from the model/source would mean creation of a duplicate query item. This duplicate query item will have name appended with number '1'. Use this as an indication to identify duplicate item and remove it.

Highlighting hidden items

We have seen that it is possible and in fact suggested to turn on the option of **Show Hidden Objects** from visual aids. This recipe will show you a best practice related to that.

Getting ready

We will use the **GO Data Warehouse (Query)** package for this. Open Cognos Report Studio and turn on the **Show Hidden Object** feature from visual aids.

How to do it...

1. Create a simple list report with **Product line**, **Product type**, and **Product name** as columns.

2. Select the **Product type** columns and turns its **Box Type** to **None**. As we have chosen to **Show Hidden Items**, we can still see the column on report page.

3. Now from the **Background Color** property, select yellow.

4. Run the report to test it.

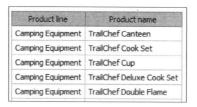

How it works...

In this recipe, we have hidden a column by changing its **Box Type**. As this item is now not going to appear on the report, we have the liberty to change its visual appearance. We changed its background color to yellow, which clearly distinguishes the item from the rest.

Next time, when any other developer opens this report in Report Studio, or when you come back to it after several weeks, you don't have to refer to any documentation or check any object property to know which items are hidden. You can just turn on the 'Show Hidden Items' feature and everything marked with yellow is part of the report but hidden in output.

This is just a development best practice to follow, which helps in maintainability. It reduces documentation need and troubleshooting time.

Relative path for images

We have seen some recipes in this book where we displayed images on the report (for example, Traffic Signal one). This recipe will show a best practice related to that.

Getting ready

We will use the report created for last recipe for this one.

How to do it...

1. Open the report in Cognos Report Studio. From **Insertable Objects | Source** pane, drag the **Product image** on list as a new column.

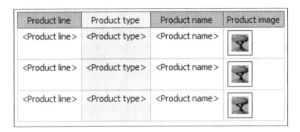

2. Run the report to test it.

   a. It is possible that the images are not displayed.

Product line	Product name	Product image
Camping Equipment	TrailChef Canteen	
Camping Equipment	TrailChef Cook Set	
Camping Equipment	TrailChef Cup	
Camping Equipment	TrailChef Deluxe Cook Set	

b. In that case, log on to the server and make sure the GO Sales sample images are located in the `{installation folder}\webcontent\samples\images` folder. If not, put them there from the sample provided with this book.

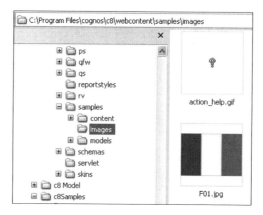

c. After putting the images in the correct folder, run the report and they should display correctly.

3. Now go back to Cognos Report Studio. Double-click on the **Product image** column. This will open the data expression window.

4. Browse the model tree from left to locate **Product image** column. Now click on the **Select Value** button to browse the values from top.

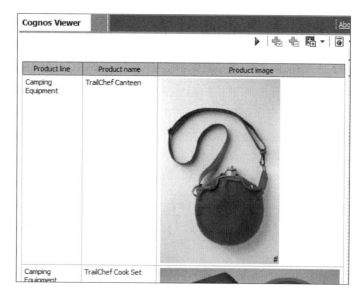

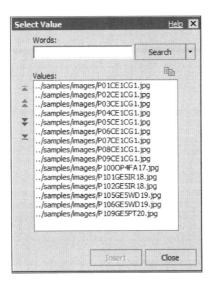

Notice that the values are Relative paths and not the Absolute paths.

5. Now let's see how it works.

How it works...

The URL of the Image object can be defined as *Absolute* or *Relative*. When we say *Relative*, it is with respect to the `Webcontent` folder within Cognos Server's installation directory.

Hence, `../samples/images/P01CE1CG1.jpg` will translate to `C:\Program Files\C8\Webcontent\samples\images\P01CE1CG1.jpg` (assuming that the installation directory on the server is `C:\Program Files\C8`).

It is best practice to always give a relative path for the images, and put the images in the `Webcontent` folder, as it allows the report to be promoted to other environments (Testing, UAT, Production, and so on) without changing any code. If we provided the absolute path, and the images were hosted on the Cognos server itself, the promotion of report to an other environment would mean that the URL of the images would need to be changed.

There's more...

It is to be noted that if you have an organization wide repository of images that are hosted on a different server to the Cognos server, you can use an Absolute path. The path won't need any change when the report is promoted to a different Cognos environment.

Taming the JavaScripts

In the 'Tips and Tricks – JavaScripts' chapter, we saw many recipes to manipulate the prompts. However, it is to be noted that JavaScripts are executed every time the page loads. Hence, it is important to control the execution of certain scripts.

This recipe will show you why taming the JavaScripts is necessary in certain cases, and how to do it.

Getting ready

We will use the report created in 'Dynamic default value for prompt' recipe (Chapter 3) for this one.

How to do it...

1. Open the report in Cognos Report Studio and save it with a different name because we are going to change it.

2. Run the report to see what it is doing. We have already written the JavaScript in this report to default the date to second entry from top, where dates are sorted from recent to old. Hence, it defaults to 200711 as per the data available in sample database.

3. Change the date to 200712 and run the report.

4. Once the report is rendered, hit the **RUN** button to re-run the report.

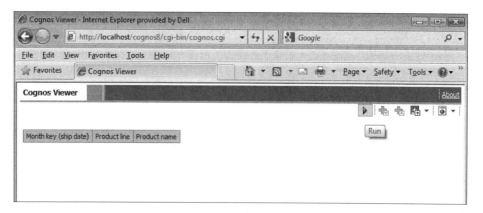

5. Notice that the date prompt goes back to 200711. This can be quite annoying especially when you have multiple prompts on the page and all of them default to certain values.

6. Close the window and go back to Cognos Report Studio.

7. Double click on the HTML item kept in report footer, beside the **Finish** button.

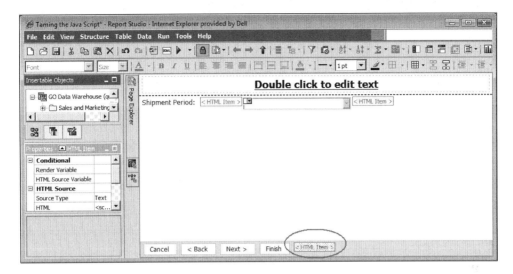

8. Replace the code, with the following:

```
<script>
function defaultSelect()
{ /* Below is the original code to change selection. We just
encompassing it in a function */
var theSpan = document.getElementById("A1");
var a = theSpan.getElementsByTagName("select");
/* This stmt return an array of all value prompts within span */
for( var i = a.length-1; i >= 0; i-- )
/* now loop through the elements */
{var prompts = a[i];
if( prompts.id.match(/PRMT_SV_/))
{      prompts.selectedIndex = 3;
}
canSubmitPrompt();
}
}
</script>
<button type="button" onclick="defaultSelect()" class="bt"
style="font-size:8pt">Apply Defaults</button>
```

9. Run the report to test it. Observe that the date prompt is now not defaulting to any value. However, there is a new button called `Apply Default` in the footer. Hit that button and date will default to second from top (that is, `200711`)

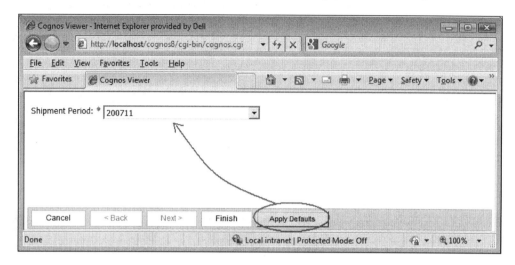

10. Change the date to `200712` and hit the **Finish** button to run the report. After the output is rendered, hit the **Run** button again and notice that the date is still `200712`. It is not automatically going back to `200711`, until we hit the **Apply Default** button.

How it works...

Here we haven't written much new code. We have just put the existing JavaScript that selects the date into a function called `defaultSelect()`. Then, we have added one line of HTML code (the `BUTTON` tag) to generate a button in the footer.

When a user clicks on the button, the function is executed, thus changing the date selection to second from top. This way we are stopping the script from automatically executing when page loads.

This is very useful when there are many prompts on the page and many of them are commonly used for known values. Users can be educated to hit the button to default those prompts to the known values, thus saving their time. Then users can over-ride the required prompt selections and on re-run, those values are retained.

Customize classes for report-wide effect

We will now see a best practice to apply standard formatting across the report and save development time at the same time.

Getting ready

Create a new report again **GO Data Warehouse (Query)** package. Pull multiple crosstabs on the report page and populate them with valid rows, columns, and measures, similar to the one shown below. Create some drill links as well.

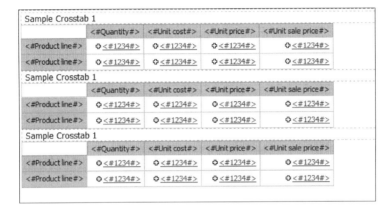

How to do it...

1. Let's work towards applying some standard formatting across the report. Open the **Page Explorer** pane and click on **Classes**.

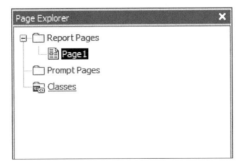

2. Locate **Crosstab member cell** from the **Global Class Extensions** list. Change its **Font** to **Bold** and **Background Colour** to **#FFCC99**.

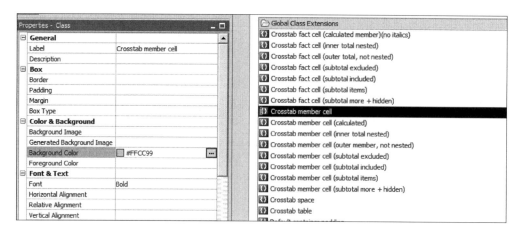

3. Similarly locate the hyperlink object and change its **Foreground Color** to black.

4. Go back to report page. Notice that the changes you made have reflected everywhere and standard formatting is applied to all **Crosstab members** and **Drill links**.

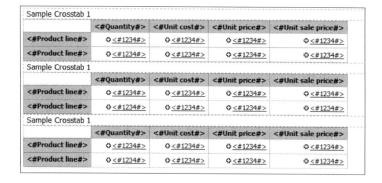

5. Run the report to test.

How it works...

The objects on the report page inherit their properties from certain classes. Report Studio allows us to modify these classes. On doing so, the changes reflect on all the objects belonging to the class. This is a better way than selecting every object and changing their properties, which is error prone.

This way we can apply standard formatting across the report and also save time.

Creating templates

In all organizations, the reporting suite is required to follow the standard formatting. Similar to other tools and technologies, Cognos Report Studio also allows you to create and use templates in order to maintain the standards, reduce cosmetic errors, and save time.

Getting ready

We will amend the report created in the previous recipe for this.

How to do it...

1. We have already defined the formatting for crosstab members and hyperlinks. Now go ahead and define standard report header and footer. You might want to put the company logo in the header.

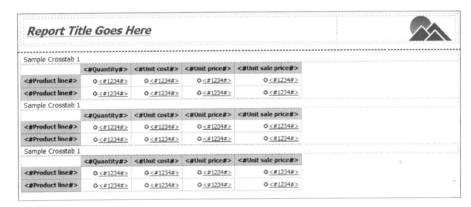

2. From the menu, Choose **File | Convert to Template**.

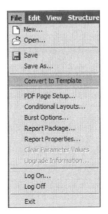

Notice that the Model/Source pane becomes empty and all data items are removed from the report.

3. From the menu, choose **File | Save As**. Give the filename as **Template**. Notice that the icon created for this 📄 is different than other reports.

4. Now we will prepare the XML specification of this template to be inserted in the server files. For that, select **Tools | Copy Report to Clipboard** from menu.

5. Go to any XML editor and paste the XML specification that we just copied. Now perform the following:

    a. From the `<report>` tag, remove the `xmlns` and `template` attributes. So it should look like this: `<report expressionLocale="en-gb">`

    b. Add a template tag just above it: `<template name= "PACKT Sample Template">`

    c. Add `</template>` at the end of the file. (Just after `</report>`)

    d. Copy the whole specification on clipboard

6. Now, on the Cognos application server, open the Cognos installation directory. Locate `C8_location/webcontent/pat/res/templates.xml` file.

7. Make a backup of the file for fail-over and then open this `templates.xml` file. Paste the specification that we copied in step 4, under `<xmlFragment id="ReportTemplates">` tag. Save the file and close it.

8. Last step is to update the `Resources.xml` file. Locate `c8_location/ webcontent/pat/res/Resources.xml` and open in XML editor.

9. Find the `<listItems>` tag. Add following line in similar fashion as the existing `<listItem>` tags.

    ```
    <listItem label="PACKT Template" icon="icon_blank.gif"
    templateName="PACKT Sample Template"/>
    ```

```
<listView id="New" view="icon" clipLabels="false">
        <listItems>
            <listItem idsLabel="IDS_LBL_NEW_BLANK_REPORT" icon="icon_blank.gif" templateName="Blank"/>
            <listItem label="PACKT Template" icon="icon_blank.gif" templateName="PACKT Sample Template"/>
            <listItem idsLabel="IDS_LBL_NEW_LIST_REPORT" icon="icon_list.gif" templateName="List"/>
            <listItem idsLabel="IDS_LBL_NEW_CROSSTAB_REPORT" icon="icon_crosstab.gif" templateName="Crosstab"
            <listItem idsLabel="IDS_LBL_NEW_CHART_REPORT" icon="icon_chart.gif" templateName="Chart"/>
            <listItem idsLabel="IDS_LBL_NEW_MAP_REPORT" icon="icon_map.gif" templateName="Map"/>
            <listItem idsLabel="IDS_LBL_NEW_FINANCIAL_REPORT" icon="icon_financial.gif" templateName="Financi
            <listItem idsLabel="IDS_LBL_NEW_REPEATER_REPORT" icon="icon_repeater.gif" templateName="Repeater"
            <listItem idsLabel="IDS_LBL_NEW_STATISTICS_REPORT" icon="icon_statistics.gif" templateName="Stati
            <listItem idsLabel="IDS_LBL_NEW_TEMPLATE_RT" icon="icon_template_qs.gif" templateName="Template_R
            <listItem idsLabel="IDS_LBL_NEW_BROWSE" icon="browse_32x32.gif" idsTooltip="IDS_TOOLTIP_NEWBROWSE
        </listItems>
</listView>
```

10. Save the file and close it.

11. Open new instance of Cognos Report Studio. Notice that a new option appears in the dialog box for **PACKT Template**.

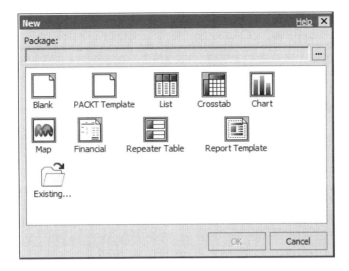

Select this option and check that the template we created initially appears.

Now you can create a new report as usual. You are rest assured that formatting of objects and other components that you placed on the templates are maintained every time you create a new report using this.

How it works...

This recipe looks like a long process but it is a one-time task which is extremely useful. We have already discussed the advantage of having templates.

If you are going to create many reports that need organization standards formatting, some common scripts and components, and generic header and footer elements—it is highly recommended that you take time to prepare a template for it.

It is common to see a Cognos developer opening one existing report, making a copy of it and then updating it—thus using the base report as template. While this serves the purpose very well, there are chances of accidently overwriting the templates. Especially in the case of multi-developer environment, it is suggested that one who has access to server installations performs this operation of defining standard template and rest of the team uses it from **New Report** dialog box.

Regression testing

The Business Intelligence or Data Warehousing and Reporting systems need on-going maintenance. New data comes in every day, volume grows, business rules change. All this can impact the existing reports structurally and performance wise. In this recipe, we will quickly see one way of doing regression test, every time anything changes in the system.

Getting ready

We will just discuss the concept here and extend the 'Timing Report Execution' recipe from the chapter 'Some More Useful Recipes'.

How to do it...

1. We saw in the 'Timing Report Execution' recipe that we can create Report View, save certain parameters for it, and then run it in the background.

2. We will now add upon this concept. For regression, you will need to create report views for each report. Save all of them in one folder.

3. Create a new job, by clicking the new job icon.

4. Add all the report views to this job. Change the **Submission of steps** to **In sequence** and **Continue on error**.

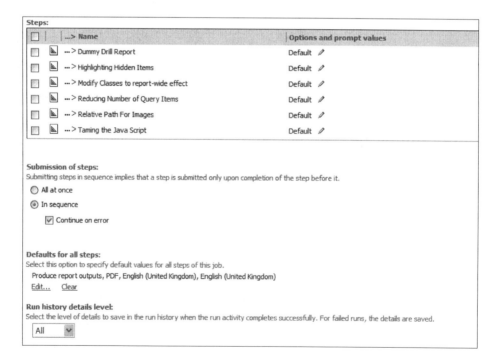

5. Change the defaults for all steps to **PDF** and **Save the Output**.

6. Save the job. Run this job every time you want to perform a regression test.

How it works...

Every time you run this job, each report view will be executed with the saved parameter values. If anything is broken structurally in the system (for example, a table or view gone missing, columns renamed, account access removed, and so on) then the execution will fail. You can refer to the **Schedule Management** or **Administration | Past Activities** from Connection Portal to check these.

Also, you can see the time taken by each report to execute. You can compare these timings with the prior runs. Thus, if the performance is affected due to any change in system (grown volume, index dropped, and so on) it will be highlighted.

It is highly recommended that you create such a mechanism in your environment and run it weekly or on-demand, to ensure that everything is working fine.

There's more...

It is possible to configure the Cognos server to produce the PDF outputs on file system. You can use this and save the outputs and compare it with a previous run to check any purposeful or accidental change impact. You will need to write a small program to rename the PDF files appropriately.

Code comments

All applications need some kind of code commenting mechanism for maintenance purposes. With programming languages it is easier; however with tools it can be a little tricky to put comments. In this recipe, we will see different options around putting comments within a report that will be invisible from users but accessible to the developers.

Getting ready

Open any existing report in Cognos Report Studio.

How to do it...

1. For the first technique to put comments and notes within a report and hide it from users, go to **Page Explorer** and create a new page. Call it **Comments**.

2. Open this new page and drag text items on it. Write all the comments about report here (description, functionality, notes, special cases, and so on).

3. Now go to **Condition Explorer** and create a new Boolean variable. Define the expression as: `1=0`. Name this variable as `Render_Comments`.

4. Go to **Comments** page. Open the **Render Variable** property and connect it to `Render_Comments` variable.

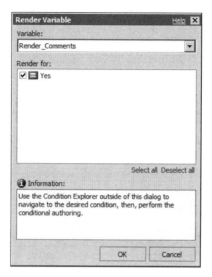

5. Run the report. Notice that **Comments** page is never rendered.

6. Now we will see another place to put comments. For that go back to Cognos Report Studio and open the main report page.

7. Drag a new **HTML item** on the report header. Define the HTML code as follows:

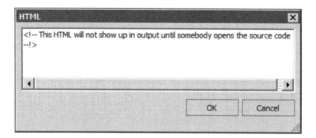

8. Run the report to test it. Notice that the comment doesn't appear in the report, but if you view the source code of the HTML output, you can see the comment.

9. Finally, let's see the XML commenting option. For that, copy the report to the clipboard.

10. Add following line in the beginning of code: `<!-- This is XML Comment -->`

```
<!-- This is XML Comment -->
<report xmlns="http://developer.cognos.com/schemas/report/6.0/" expressionLocale="en-gb">
                        <modelPath>/content/package[@name='GO Finance Cube']/model[@nam
                        <drillBehavior modelBasedDrillThru="true"/>
```

11. Copy the whole specification again and paste it back into Cognos Report Studio. Save the report.

12. Run the report to test it.

How it works...

We have seen three ways of putting comments and notes within report in this recipe. All of them work fine and do their job.

Some developers don't like creating a new page or HTML item for storing the comments, as this means creating some objects on the report that are not required. These objects form a part of the XML specification and they are validated and parsed every time the report runs.

Following that belief, we can put the comments in the XML specification itself. That way comments are completely ignored by the Studio while validating and parsing. However, it does mean that each time the developer needs to refer to or update the comments; he will have to copy the report specification in XML editor.

Having a separate page (first approach) is a very clean method. However, it doesn't allow you to put comments in-line. So if you have a comment or note specific to a column or prompt, you can't just put it near that object and make it noticeable.

I personally find the HTML comment method to be the best. By having one HTML item in the page header, I can put all the commentary about that page in there. Also, I can create specific HTML items to hold particular object related notes and put it near that object. Also, later on, if I am running any report and want to see the comments, I don't have to open it in Cognos Report Studio. Instead, I can just look at the HTML Source Code and it will have those comments inline.

I will leave it to your own experiments and preference to decide which one to follow in your team.

Recommendations and References

In this chapter, we will cover the following topics:

- ▶ Version controlling
- ▶ Recommendation for Prompt types
- ▶ The Cognos mash-up service
- ▶ Third party tools for Cognos
- ▶ Express Authoring mode
- ▶ CAFÉ
- ▶ Cognos Go Office

Introduction

Let us now see some topics that are very useful for a Cognos report developer to know about.

Version controlling

Cognos allows direct connection to certain version controlling software (Visual Source Safe being the most popular) for Framework Manager. However, there is no direct mechanism for the reports.

The following methods are seen in different organizations for Version Controlling of the reports:

- ▶ Copy the report specification to clipboard, save it as an XML file, and store it in the version controlling system.

❏ This method allows easy comparison to prior versions of the report, and hence is good for code review during any changes.

❏ However, it can be tedious. Also, restoring to older version needs to be done one report at a time. This also breaks any existing report views defined at the target location.

▸ Export the whole suite of report and store the export file (ZIP format) in the version controlling system.

❏ This is less tedious than prior one as only one file is created for whole suite of reports.

❏ Reverting back to an older and stable state is easy. (Entire suite is reverted back so you can bring the system back to older and stable state – like baseline)

❏ However, this method is not particularly useful while troubleshooting a report to check what changed in it over the versions.

▸ Use of third party tools.

❏ It is possible to hook up to the content store to retrieve the information. There are some third-party tools available that use this method to retrieve report specification and do certain jobs.

❏ You can consider the tools like MotioCI to automatically record the report versions and track changes. They also allow you to revert to older versions. (More information can be found on: `http://www.motio.com/products/ci/overview.do`)

Recommendation for prompt types

There are many types of prompts available for use in Cognos Report Studio. Let's see some information about when to use which kind of prompt.

Data	Suggested prompt	Information
Hierarchical	Tree prompt	This naturally supports the hierarchical data
Two to four values – Single select, mandatory	Radio Button group	The value prompt can be used in Radio Button UI for this kind of requirement
Five to hundred values – Single select	Drop Down list	This is another UI of value prompt. It saves space on the prompt page.
Five to hundred values – Multi select	List box	This UI of value prompt allows users to select multiple values by holding *Shift* and *Ctrl* keys

Data	Suggested prompt	Information
More than hundred values	Search and Select prompt	When more than one hundred distinct values are available to choose from, it is advisable to use this prompt as user can search for required values which are simpler than browsing. Also, it reduces the burden to populate all values when prompt loads.

Cognos Mashup Service

The Cognos Mashup Service is a web service that ships along with Cognos SDK (Software Development Kit) for version 8.4.1 onwards. While Cognos SDK supports report authoring through programming, the Mashup Service is purely meant to run the reports, access the report output, and expose the contents to other business applications in UI and workflow.

Partner Services talk to **Cognos Mashup Service** (**CMS**) using REST or SOAP request. The contents are accessed in XML, LDX, HTML, or JSON format. You can find more information about this on the IBM developerWorks Library.

Some popular usages of CMS are embedding Cognos Report contents into Google Maps, Google Earth, Adobe Air, and so on. For example: http://www.ibm.com/developerworks/data/library/cognos/page486.html

You can find more information and examples on the IBM developerWorks and other discussion forums.

Third-party tools for Cognos

As Cognos provides a very open structure and easy access to contents and components through SDK and CMS, there are many products built over it. They use Cognos as the powerful application engine to generate the contents and then these tools present the contents in very stylist way. When just Cognos Report Studio can not meet your business requirement, you can consider using such third-party tools to enhance the Cognos services and extract more value out of the investment made in Cognos.

An example of such a tool is **AV Dashboard** (product owned by INCA Software). This tool gives visual representation of data using embedded reporting. With animated visuals, maps, tickers, charts, transitions, and so on, this tool gives a refreshing and interesting access to information. With the ability to export to PowerPoint, it makes a good choice for business users who need it for presentations and marketing.

(Website: `http://www.incasoftware.co.uk/en/1/avdashboard.html`)

Another tool called **Xcelsius** can be used on the top of Cognos output to provide a cute interface in Flash and PowerPoint. This is a SAP product and more information can be found here: `http://www.sap.com/solutions/sapbusinessobjects/sme/reporting-dashboarding/xcelsius/index.epx`

Sometimes even developers come out with small but useful utilities—a great example is: **PimpMyReport** (`http://pimpmyreport.appspot.com`). This is an online tool that allows you to parse the XML specification of report and generate a quick documentation within no time. This cute little application can save your documentation time.

The following is a screenshot of PimpMyReport. All you need to do is 'Copy Report to Clipboard' from Report Studio which in turn copies the XML specification. Paste it into the website and hit the button. Within no time, it will list out all the data items and filters with their expressions—for your documentation purpose.

Above tool is free. However, if you want more sophisticated documentations, you might want to purchase **SpecStudio** from **Assimil8** (Website: http://www.assimil8.com/Featured-Product.aspx). This website offers a free trial wherein you can submit the report XML and the document will be mailed back to you.

Motio is one more company that has several products to help in Cognos Development. These products talk directly to Cognos servers and content manager and provide some functionalities that Cognos tools don't. This suite includes a tool called **MotioADF** which is an Application Development Framework and the company claims it to be faster and more reliable than developing using Cognos SDK. (Website: `http://www.motio.com/products.do`)

You can use such tools to aid the Cognos Report Development lifecycle, reduce defects, and improve maintainability.

Express Authoring Mode

As IT becomes wide spread, business users are becoming more and more IT aware. The new generation of business analysts, managers, executives are not scared of complicated looking applications. They are keen to take the driving seat and try things themselves rather than relying on IT staff for their data and information needs.

That is why IBM now provides Cognos Report Studio with a special mode called 'Express Authoring Mode'. This is a simplified reporting interface designed for non-technical users to quickly create traditional style reports.

You can start **Express Authoring Mode** in Report Studio by choosing the option from **View** menu.

This mode works only with Dimensional and Dimensionally Modeled Relational schema/ sources. It allows you create only crosstab style reports and populates data on the report page as you drag objects on it.

This is similar to Analysis Studio, however gives more flexibility around Report formatting and styling. Also it has more features than Query Studio, making it a tool of choice.

CAFE

IBM's **Cognos Analysis For Excel** (**CAFE**) tool is quickly becoming popular among business and financial analysts. This Excel add-in is separately sold by IBM (doesn't ship with BI installation) and needs to be installed on the users' machines. It enables the users to directly perform analysis in Excel with Cognos sitting as a layer between data source and Excel.

Cognos Framework Model works as the modeling and security layer here. It allows multiple data sources to be pulled together in one business layer which is exposed in Excel using CAFÉ. Users can directly perform drag-n-drop, slice-n-dice operations to analyze the data.

They can put Excel calculations like forecast on top of the figures and also create Excel charts etc. This brings the benefits of Cognos and Excel together and makes a killer application.

I would strongly recommend CAFÉ is your organization has data analysts who need to ad-hoc analysis over data from warehouse and various other sources. You would need strong data modeling skills and this logic will sit in Framework Model. CAFÉ is suitable for dimensional models and **Dimensionally Modeled Relational** (**DMR**) schemas.

A screenshot of how CAFÉ looks is shown below:

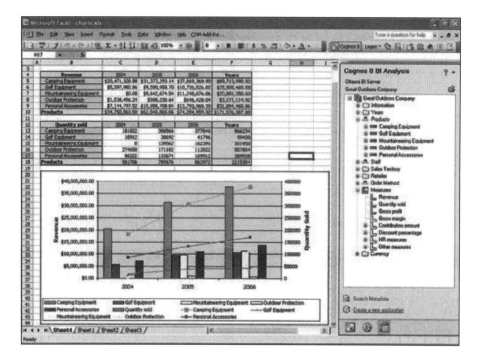

More information about CAFÉ can be found on the IBM website.

Cognos Go Office

CAFE that allows you to do data analysis in Excel, can be just too smart for the business users. Probably they only want to pull the contents of pre-defined reports on their spreadsheets, Word documents, or PowerPoint presentations.

Then Cognos Go Office is the way the go. It allows users to pull the contents like graphs, charts, tables, and crosstabs from existing reports in their MS Office documents. They can refresh the contents on demand. More information can be found on the IBM website: http://www-01.ibm. com/software/data/cognos/products/cognos-8-go/

Index

Thank you for buying
IBM Cognos 8 Report Studio Cookbook

About Packt Publishing

Packt, pronounced 'packed', published its first book "Mastering phpMyAdmin for Effective MySQL Management" in April 2004 and subsequently continued to specialize in publishing highly focused books on specific technologies and solutions.

Our books and publications share the experiences of your fellow IT professionals in adapting and customizing today's systems, applications, and frameworks. Our solution based books give you the knowledge and power to customize the software and technologies you're using to get the job done. Packt books are more specific and less general than the IT books you have seen in the past. Our unique business model allows us to bring you more focused information, giving you more of what you need to know, and less of what you don't.

Packt is a modern, yet unique publishing company, which focuses on producing quality, cutting-edge books for communities of developers, administrators, and newbies alike. For more information, please visit our website: www.packtpub.com.

About Packt Enterprise

In 2010, Packt launched two new brands, Packt Enterprise and Packt Open Source, in order to continue its focus on specialization. This book is part of the Packt Enterprise brand, home to books published on enterprise software – software created by major vendors, including (but not limited to) IBM, Microsoft and Oracle, often for use in other corporations. Its titles will offer information relevant to a range of users of this software, including administrators, developers, architects, and end users.

Writing for Packt

We welcome all inquiries from people who are interested in authoring. Book proposals should be sent to author@packtpub.com. If your book idea is still at an early stage and you would like to discuss it first before writing a formal book proposal, contact us; one of our commissioning editors will get in touch with you.

We're not just looking for published authors; if you have strong technical skills but no writing experience, our experienced editors can help you develop a writing career, or simply get some additional reward for your expertise.

IBM Cognos 8 Planning

ISBN: 978-1-847196-84-2   Paperback: 424 pages

Engineer a clear-cut strategy for achieving best-in-class results

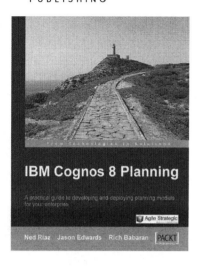

1. Build and deploy effective planning models using Cognos 8 Planning

2. Filled with ideas and techniques for designing planning models

3. Ample screenshots and clear explanations to facilitate learning

4. Written for first-time developers focusing on what is important to the beginner

Learning SQL Server 2008 Reporting Services

ISBN: 978-1-847196-18-7   Paperback: 512 pages

A step-by-step guide to getting the most of Microsoft SQL Server Reporting Services 2008

1. Everything you need to create and deliver data-rich reports with SQL Server 2008 Reporting Services as quickly as possible

2. Packed with hands-on-examples to learn and improve your skills

3. Connect and report from databases, spreadsheets, XML Data, and more

4. No experience of SQL Server Reporting Services required

Please check **www.PacktPub.com** for information on our titles

JasperReports for Java Developers

ISBN: 978-1-904811-90-9   Paperback: 344 pages

Create, Design, Format and Export Reports with the world's most popular Java reporting library

1. Get started with JasperReports, and develop the skills to get the most from it

2. Create, design, format, and export reports

3. Generate report data from a wide range of datasources

4. Integrate Jasper Reports with Spring, Hibernate, Java Server Faces, or Struts

Practical Data Analysis and Reporting with BIRT

ISBN: 978-1-847191-09-0   Paperback: 312 pages

Use the open-source Eclipse-based Business Intelligence and Reporting Tools system to design and create reports quickly

1. Get started with BIRT Report Designer

2. Develop the skills to get the most from it

3. Transform raw data into visual and interactive content

3. Design, manage, format, and deploy high-quality reports

Please check **www.PacktPub.com** for information on our titles

1545787R0

Printed in Great Britain by
Amazon.co.uk, Ltd.,
Marston Gate.